Priscilla Cooper Tyler

Priscilla Cooper Tyler

AND THE AMERICAN SCENE

1816-1889

By ELIZABETH TYLER COLEMAN

UNIVERSITY OF ALABAMA PRESS

Manufactured in the United States of America

∞
The paper on which this book is printed meets the minimum requirements of American National Standard for Information Science—Permanence of Paper for Printed Library Materials, ANSI Z39.48-1984.

First paperback printing, 2006

Library of Congress Control Number 55005625

IN MEMORY OF

VIRGINIA SCOTT COLEMAN

FOREWORD

THIS BIOGRAPHY OF PRISCILLA COOPER TYLER is based largely on original manuscripts collected under the auspices of the Research Committee of the University of Alabama and now deposited as the Cooper Papers in the University of Alabama Library.

Thomas A. Cooper, the distinguished early nineteenth-century actor, his wife, Mary Fairlie Cooper, and their many children lived in or near the vortex of a variety of social, political, and cultural movements of their day and commented indefatigably on all they saw and experienced. It is unfortunate that so few of their writings have survived the hazard of time, for those which have been preserved are tantalizing evidence of a wealth of lost material. Of Cooper's life-long friendship with William Godwin and Mary Shelley, for instance, there is but a single note; of what he wrote to Dunlap, Wignell, Stone, Wood, Sol Smith, and other actors and managers important in the early American theatre, little remains. Mary Fairlie Cooper's lively correspondence with Irving is represented by only one letter. Probably the most interesting of the documents in the collection are Mary Grace Cooper's diary, kept while on tour with her father, and a journal and a number of letters written by Priscilla Cooper Tyler while she was on the stage and in the White House.

Heedless about preserving priceless manuscripts, the Coopers were likewise careless about other matters. They seemed reluctant to waste a moment of their lives in achieving elegance of penmanship, their handwritings suggesting less interest in the way the page looked than in crowding every inch of the paper with interesting information. They frequently crossed and recrossed lines, at times using initials for proper names—sometimes blanks, if a scandal or a romance were involved. Liberal use of sealing wax often blotted out words and sentences on the opposite side of the sheet. They were, moreover, quite casual in dating their correspondence; consequently chronology had to be determined largely by content.

These facts made the task of interpreting the material so bewildering that, without the help of those familiar with family history, the papers could never have been put in order. Louisa Tyson, Grace Tyson Gatewood, T. Gardner Foster, Priscilla Foster Stevenson, Priscilla Goodwyn Griffin, grandchildren of Priscilla the First, have furnished guidance. They have, moreover, donated many of the most valuable documents included in the collection. Grace Lane, Letitia Arant, Ellie and John Scott, Irene Armistead, Frances Hails, Carolyn M. Schley, and Matilda M. Nelson, all representatives or connections of the widely scattered descendants of Thomas A. Cooper, have likewise made valuable contributions. Frank Charles opened up for examination boxes of old manuscripts in the attic at Chantilly; and Sue Ruffin Tyler furnished typed copies of material collected by the late Lyon G. Tyler. The family circle and friends have been so generous that the task of collecting and editing the one hundred or so letters and three journals that comprise the Cooper Papers has presented no really baffling problems.

Much more difficult was selecting one of the many arresting personalities represented in the material to be the central figure of this study; and though the decision finally rested on Priscilla Cooper Tyler, it has not always been easy to let her keep the center of the stage. Her sister, Mary Grace Raoul, unselfish and self-effacing, threatened at times to claim more interest than was fair to the heroine of the story. Thomas Cooper, Priscilla's father; John Tyler, her father-in-law; and Robert Tyler, her husband, frequently crowded her out of the spotlight. But this is a situation for which she herself must be held accountable. The dramatic story of her life is really the story of those she loved. She identified herself with them so completely that they controlled her destiny; it is no wonder then that they at times dominate her biography.

Throughout the editing of the Cooper Papers and the other details of making this book, W. Stanley Hoole, director of libraries of the University of Alabama, and Vivien M. Lawson, head of the Reference Department, have been most kind to me. Dr. Hoole and Dr. Frank L. Owsley, head of the Department of History of the University of Alabama, have offered helpful suggestions. Katherine Vickery of Montevallo did considerable research for me in New Orleans libraries. And, lastly, I am deeply indebted to Murial Williams, who has been secretary and encouraging friend throughout the two years which I have devoted to the Cooper Family.

ELIZABETH TYLER COLEMAN

University of Alabama
Summer, 1954

CONTENTS

ILLUSTRATIONS

1

CHILDHOOD IN NEW YORK

1816-1819

ELIZABETH PRISCILLA COOPER, the second daughter and third child of Thomas A. Cooper[1] and Mary Fairlie Cooper, was born in New York City, June 14, 1816. The romantic marriage of her parents four years before had been a nine days wonder among the class-conscious aristocracy of the young republic. Her mother, Mary Fairlie, was at that time the acknowledged belle of the assemblies, not only at home but in Boston and Philadelphia as well.[2] She had captured the attention, if not the heart, of the most sought-after of bachelors, Washington Irving, who made her a celebrity by putting her into *Salamagundi Papers* as "Sophie Sparkle" and by quoting her epigrams. There he described her as "a young lady unrivaled for playful wit and innocent vivacity . . . who like a brilliant adds lustre to the front of fashion."[3]

This extravagant praise was considered an understatement by her mother's and father's friends—the Hosacks, the Livingstons, the Kembles, the Hoffmans, the Brevoorts, the Gouverneur Morrises, and other elegant gentlefolk who enjoyed the hospitality of the mansion at 41 Cortlandt Street.[4] The older and more conservative among these good people wagged their heads sadly and wondered what the world was coming to when Major Fairlie's daughter, descended on her mother's side from the Yateses and the Van Nesses, married an actor.[5] Their disapproval of the match was unaffected by the fact that they had entertained the bridegroom in their homes and had introduced him to their wives and daughters. They acknowledged Cooper's gentlemanly bearing, his social graces, his integrity, his distinction as the outstanding star on the American stage and able manager of the Park Theatre; but a deeply rooted prejudice they themselves could not have explained made them sympathize with Major and Mrs. Fairlie, who did not attend the wedding, and condone the rudeness of Mary's elder brother in refusing to speak to the bridegroom.[6]

As for Mary Livingston, Ann Hoffman, Margaret Brevoort, and that scatterbrain, Maria Laight—Mary Fairlie's intimates and contemporaries—there was probably no one of these girls who would not have changed places with the bride.[7] Cooper, aged thirty-six, with more good looks and more reckless charm than one man has a right to, had fluttered the pulse of many a susceptible maiden who came to the theatre to admire him in *Hamlet* and *Macbeth* and to sigh for him in romantic parts like Barnwell.

The admiration of these charmers, expressed largely in faithful attendance at plays in which he starred, Cooper accepted with impersonal courtesy. Being a widower whose first marriage had not been a happy one, he had been rather cynical about women until he was attracted to Mary Fairlie. Indifferent to ambitious hostesses who sought to "lionize" him, he greatly preferred masculine society. Before he fell in love he had sought out as companions the young men of the *beau monde*—the Irving brothers, James Kirk Paulding, Richard McCall, Henry Brevoort, Henry Ogden—who as patrons of the arts frequented the Green Room at the Park, and as friends came often to the double house occupied by Cooper and his partner, Stephen Price. There they enjoyed good talk, good wine, and playing cards for high stakes.[8] This group thought Cooper was taking, as he often did, a gambler's chance in courting Mary Fairlie and never dreamed that he could win her.

During 1808-1812, Washington Irving, being addicted to gossip about notables, wrote frequent bulletins to his many correspondents in regard to the progress of what he called the "siege of Mary"[9] and expressed great surprise when after three years she finally capitulated.[10]

In spite of family disapproval and prognostications of friends to the contrary, the couple were married in June of 1812 and left immediately for a honeymoon in South Carolina.[11] Cooper had in all things a passion for preeminence, so he must have felt pride in introducing his new wife to the Alfred Hugers, the Coghills, the Raouls, to J. B. Irving and Henry Gourdin, his personal friends and admirers in and around Charleston and Columbia.[12] She possessed the beauty and the distinction which Joanna Cooper, his first wife, had lacked,[13] and doubtless met with the warm approval of the discriminating plantation aristocracy of the South.

By the time the bride and groom returned, they had ceased to be the principal topic of conversation around fashionable tea tables in New York and were allowed to settle down to domesticity in comparative privacy. The Fairlies for the most part tried to make the best of what they were always to consider a bad bargain; and when in 1816 Priscilla was born, the domestic harmony which prevailed in the Coopers' handsome establishment on the corner of Leonard and Broadway seemed proof to everyone concerned of the success of the marriage. Even before the advent of this third child, the nursery there was comfortably filled by Mary Grace and James Fairlie, born in 1813 and 1814 respectively. No matter what latent antagonisms divided the family, parents and grandparents, uncles and aunts had achieved solidarity in their devotion to "Mary's children."

Only Maria Fairlie, Mary Fairlie Cooper's mother, refused to compromise. She was barely civil to her actor son-in-law. She resented the fact that he was not like the men she had been accustomed to admire and respect. Her father, Chief Justice Yates, had been a distinguished jurist, a member of the Convention of 1787, a man of influence, whose stand in regard to the ratification of the Constitution by New York (1787-1788) had aligned him with Governor Clinton against Hamilton, Madison, and Jay.[14] His opponents had won the public over by the masterly arguments expressed in *The Federalist,* but Robert Yates's had been an honorable defeat, one that had established his reputation as having played a small but important part in the brief history of the United States of America.

Maria did not think that Tom Cooper—who had not come to the New World from England until he was twenty—could hold a candle to such a patriot as her father or to such a gallant soldier as her husband, Major James Fairlie, who had been during the Revolution Baron Steuben's favorite among the young officers on his staff. Fairlie had been called "Handsome Jem" by his comrades-in-arms and had enjoyed among them modest fame, not only for his courage in battle but for having made the Commander-in-Chief, General Washington, laugh outright. After the war, as claim agent and clerk of the Supreme Court of New York, he earned a salary sufficient to support his wife and five children in luxury[15] and to entertain distinguished visitors from abroad, such as Talleyrand and Joseph Bonaparte, who frequently dined at his home.[16]

Maria Yates Fairlie, worthy daughter and dutiful wife, assumed the right to be critical of those who wished to marry into the dynasty. When she was an old woman she confessed that pride had always been her besetting sin.[17] And indeed her conviction that the Fairlies, the Yateses, and her mother's family, the Van Nesses, were superior to the rest of mankind may have been responsible for the fact that her two sons, John and Nicholas, died bachelors and that Louisa, her eldest daughter, though the poet Halleck courted her assiduously, remained an old maid.[18] Julia, the youngest of the girls, refused many suitors and finally, in spite of her mother's mockery of "Cupid in spectacles,"[19] married a man much older than she, Samuel Gouveneur Ogden. All three of the girls were beautiful and witty, and the boys are said to have been not without their share of the family's good looks, but only Mary and Julia married—both in opposition to their mother's wishes.

No one within the sphere of Maria Fairlie's influence was unaffected by the power of her personality and the strength of her will. Her disapproval of Thomas Cooper, which strengthened with the decline of his prosperity, was to create a problem for Mary Fairlie Cooper and her children. It was especially to affect Priscilla, who, resentful of the Fairlies' attitude toward her father, was to grow up feeling that the discord in the family circle was of her grandmother's making, and to side with Cooper in all differences. And yet, when she was called upon in later years to play the part of a queen on the stage or to receive ambassadors in her official capacity as mistress of the White House, she imitated her grandmother's "old fashioned curtseys such as must have existed in the days of the Empire,"[20] and tried to achieve Maria Fairlie's combination of dignity and graciousness.

During the years of their residence in New York the Cooper children were too young to be aware of antagonisms within the family; Priscilla was only three when they left in 1819; Mary Grace and Jim, not much older. Tradition has preserved for three generations anecdotes which suggest that they were happy and free from inhibitions. After all, Tom Cooper had been brought up by a radical thinker, who had decided convictions in regard to the danger of ill-advised discipline. His foster father was William Godwin, later the husband of Mary Wollstonecraft and the father of Mary Shelley. Godwin, a bachelor at the time, was living in Surrey, England, when a cousin, Hannah Cooper, to whom he was indebted for kindness, was left destitute by the death of her husband. Moved by genuine compassion as well as by a desire to experiment with Rousseau's theories, then current in education, he offered to adopt nine-year-old Tom, the most promising of Hannah's three children. The young philosopher was at work on his masterpiece, *Political Justice,* a treatise which held that if the state allowed liberty enough, vice could not exist. In bringing up Cooper, Godwin assumed that a similar principle applied in rearing a child: that a boy given his freedom would be good and happy.

There must have been times when adherence to this doctrine was difficult in dealing with his protege, who did not fit perfectly into any pattern of behavior. The teacher learned as well as taught in the fearless interchange of insult that often went on between them. Strangely enough, neither party to the experiment considered abandoning it; they fought their way through to mutual respect and affection. C. Kegan Paul in his biography, *William Godwin: His Friends and Contemporaries,* gives an excellent account of how Cooper, as rebellious as a wild colt, was tamed without having his spirit broken. The boy grew up honorable, proud, and passionate. He spurned mediocrity, and, determining to be a hero at any price, decided at sixteen upon the stage as a career. *Aut Caesar, aut nihil* was his personal motto as he fought his way, in spite of the petty jealousies of fellow actors and the tyranny of managers, to success at Covent Garden and eventually to stardom in America.[21] The mature Thomas Cooper had every reason to feel that Godwin's unconventional methods had prepared him for the vicissitudes of life; for by the time his children were born, he was riding the high tide of fame and fortune. He therefore advocated for his son and even for his daughters freedom such as he had known, and he approved the leniency of Mary's rule, though some of their friends thought her too mild and permisssive a mother.

On one occasion a matron, sitting genteelly in the drawing room making small talk, heard in the room overhead a sudden tumult of wild screams and running feet. Alarmed, she exclaimed, "Aren't you going up to them?"

"No," said Mary seriously, "I never go until I hear a body being *dragged*."[22] Her jesting remark was more than half in earnest. Tom Cooper's offspring worked out their destinies successfully with a minimum of parental interference.

The ultimate result of this policy was admirable; but, according to family chronicles, Priscilla at first reflected little credit on her upbringing. In later years she always denied the legend that when she was three she threw a pack of playing cards in Irving's face because she thought he gave himself airs. Reasonably enough, she pointed out that he left America in 1815, before she was born, and did not return until 1832, when she was too old for such behavior. She agreed, however, that there was some foundation for the scandal, since she was always provoked to irreverence by those who took their importance too seriously. She admitted that although the victim of her naughtiness was not Irving, it might well have been any one of the guests who came to her mother and father's home.

Not entirely in harmony with these tales but equally apocryphal is a statement made by Joe Cowell in his book of reminiscences, *Thirty Years Among the Players,* that the children were from the first taught self-control by their father:

> "He used to boast of never allowing his children to cry. 'Sir, when my children were young and began to cry, I always dashed a glass of water in their faces, and that so astonished them that they would leave off; and if they began again, I'd dash another, and keep increasing the dose till they were entirely cured'."

Cowell asserts that this unique method of correction was partly responsible for Priscilla's "affable but dignified deportment" in later life.[23]

Cooper was anxious that his boy and his girls grow up sturdy, with health as robust as his own; so he insisted that they exercise in the fresh air, and on one occasion decreed that Mary Grace and Priscilla be encouraged to play in the rain in their slips. Their mother thought this going too far, for such immodest exposure would be censured in the fashionable neighborhood where they lived. Little ladies, convention decreed, stayed indoors when it rained, and even on fair days wore a multiplicity of garments when they rolled their hoops in Battery Park.[24]

Cooper took his duties as a father so seriously and made so many revolutionary suggestions about his children's upbringing that it was just as well he was gone for months at a time. In the spring and in the fall he left to make the circuit through the South and the West, where his services as a star were eagerly sought. When he was in New York, he spent long hours in rehearsal or business. Twice a week he posted over impossible roads to Philadelphia. Heedless in the regulation of his personal affairs, he was meticulous about the business of running the Park Theatre. He and his partner, Stephen Price, a theatrical manager well and favorably known on both sides of the Atlantic, had spent $15,000 to make it the most luxurious playhouse in the city—with coffee rooms, mirrors, light purple panels, gold moldings, and crimson draperies.[25]

Mary Grace, Jim, and Priscilla probably sat with their mother behind the velvet curtains of Cooper's private box and watched their father act, but they were too young to realize the experience fully. More to their liking was the drama of his frequent exits and entrances at home. They must have been excited when his costume trunks were loaded onto the especially constructed gig in which he drove himself on his many journeys. He was proud of his horsemanship and would slap the reins on the backs of the two shining horses, hitched tandem, and start for Boston, Pittsburgh, or New Orleans as if he faced adventure instead of hardship. To see him set out with confidence and return in triumph never became a matter of course to Mary or to the children.[26]

When he went South and took along a trotting horse or a hunting dog, the family were eager to know the outcome of the fantastic wagers he placed on his favorites. It was no secret that he indulged with the Charleston and New York aristocracy in what is known as "the gentlemanly vice"—and he usually won, for he was fortune's favorite in those days. Abstinent in the matter of strong drink, he liked to show his indifference to the vast sums he earned by recklessness at the card table, or, for that matter, betting on anything—the weight of a friend, the height of a room, the outcome of an election.[27] All losses he incurred he took lightly. On one occasion he bet the proceeds of his benefit performance ($1200) that he could pull a longer straw from a passing hay wagon than Price could. When he lost, he laughed. "It's only two hours' acting," he said.[28]

Sometimes his endurance rather than his luck was the deciding factor in a bet. Once he undertook to walk to Baltimore from

Philadelphia in less time than a friend could ride without change of horse. "This wager he won with little exertion, arriving in fit condition to act that evening."[29]

There is no evidence to indicate that in 1819 Cooper's splendid strength was failing, or that he had met with financial disaster which made it wise to abandon the extravagance of keeping up the New York establishment. His relationship with Price was harmonious; business at the Park was good; no especial discord with the Fairlies occasioned a crisis. Nevertheless he decided to give up his managership of the theatre and move to some small town. He was master in his own home, and no one questioned him, least of all Priscilla, who had no voice as yet in any decision. A very small satellite in the galaxy swayed by the great star, her fate as well as that of her mother and the other children depended entirely upon Cooper, who, in his turn, seems to have accepted as his destiny what pride or ambition or chance prompted him to do at the moment.

2

GIRLHOOD IN BRISTOL

1819-1833

ANY NUMBER of reasons might be suggested why Bristol, Pennsylvania, was a reasonable choice for the Coopers' new home. Because of nearby Bath Springs the place enjoyed local fame as a health resort. Moreover, it was accessible, for the old post road between New York and Philadelphia, places where Cooper most often had business, passed through the heart of the town. Tradition has it that chance played an important part in his determination to establish his family there. One night in Paris, he was playing for high stakes and won everything his opponent risked, including a pleasant cottage with a garden that sloped down to the Delaware River.[1] After his return home he asked his wife how she would like to live in a village and brought her to see the new property. Mary Fairlie Cooper fell in love with the house and the old town. She liked its remoteness from the noise and strife of cities, the lure of far-away places suggested by the sailing vessels that lay at anchor in the river, the air of gentle decay which gave it atmosphere. A professed Romantic, she saw it in terms of poems like Gray's "Elegy" and "The Deserted Village."

Bristol, called Buckingham by early settlers, had a history, the days of its glory being during and just after the period when Philadelphia was the capital of the nation. At that time numbers of dignitaries like the Spanish ambassador, Señor de

Onis, or Baron Ludwig of Prussia, built homes on Radcliffe Street on the banks of the river. They were attracted not only by the beautiful surroundings but by the reputation of Bath Springs, where the fashionable world flocked to drink the medicinal waters. After the turn of the century the fickle public found Saratoga or Balston more to its liking. The Springs near Bristol were deserted, the race track closed, and the town gave itself to memories of departed glory.

There were still a few distinguished foreign residents, but most of the inhabitants were substantial Quaker folk. Down by the wharf lived seafaring men, who reloaded the coal brought from the mines onto outgoing boats and transported it to distant ports. The arrival and departure of this prosaic cargo created a brief stir in the idyllic calm, as did the coming of the stage wagon with its backless seats, which daily stopped at the door of the Delaware House. There was always a group of the idle or the curious assembled to stare at the travellers who dismounted to ease their cramped muscles and refresh themselves with the excellent food and drink served by the host of the old inn. These events were ripples on the quietly flowing life of the community into which the Coopers came in 1819.[2]

Not since Major Lenox, once ambassador to the Court of St. James, built the Keene Mansion three years before, had there been so much excitement as there was at the news that Thomas A. Cooper, famous star of the American stage, was bringing his wife and three children to live at 722 Radcliffe Street. There was much talk after the family moved in about the grandeur of the drawing-room, hung with Gobelin tapestries.[3] A number of people thought the handsome actor, now at the height of his fame and good looks, was like the Byronic heroes in the novels they read; and his wife like the sweet and yielding heroines. After a decent interval the gentry came to call and later sent their children to play with Mary Grace, James Fairlie, and Elizabeth Priscilla. Captain and Mrs. Meyers, whose daughters were just the ages of the Cooper girls; Mr. and Mrs. Bache, whose children were too well brought up to boast that they were descendants of the great Franklin's only daughter; Dr. and Mrs. Phillips, highly respected in the community; Dr. and Mrs. McIllvain, whose brother was Bishop McIllvain; Mr. and Mrs. Riche, whose Juliana was to be Jim Cooper's first sweetheart—all these good people were from first acquaintance attracted to the Coopers, nor did the friendships dating from these years lapse even when the older generation had passed away and the children were widely scattered.

The most unusual of the visitors was the Emperor Napoleon's brother, Joseph Bonaparte, once King of Naples and King of Spain. He lived on a fine estate at Burlington in style befitting exiled royalty. The little Coopers thought it a splendid sight to see him, accompanied by his nephew, Prince Murat, come down the river in a barge, rowed by four oarsmen, with flags flying fore and aft.[4] On his very first visit to the family he held Priscilla on his knee and seemed at home with the household. Years later, when he left for France, he gave Tom Cooper a bust of Napoleon, which was a treasured heirloom for many generations.

After only one year's residence in their charming cottage, Cooper bought the lot next door and built a house in which the children, their governess, and their nurse were installed, while he and Mary stayed in the first home.[5] This remarkable experiment—one family under two roofs, with a covered causeway between—proved a wise investment in comfort and convenience; for Priscilla did not long enjoy the distinction of being the baby in the household. She was crowded out of that privileged position by the arrival in quick succession of four additional sisters.[6] No wonder Mary Grace, an earnest, well-behaved little girl, took her seniority seriously. In the course of time she became the model to be emulated by Olivia, Julia, Virginia, and Louisa. She felt called upon to set them an excellent example of diligence in the pursuit of knowledge and industry at household tasks—an example the volatile Priscilla found admirable but impossible to emulate. Although hers was a cheerful presence in the schoolroom of "the White House," as the children called their quarters, her influence was not always good. On at least one occasion, notable in family history, she rebelled against the authority vested in Miss Hannah, the governess.[7] A tremendous tempest, of more than teapot proportions, was precipitated by Priscilla's bland announcement that she never intended to learn the multiplication tables. Shocked surprise greeted her declaration; her misconduct was reported to her father, who called her into his study for reprimand. Even when the scene with him assumed some of the dramatic intensity of Lear's arraignment of Cordelia, his rebellious daughter maintained her right to ignorance. Her father in the end came to respect her firmness and concluded that after all there was no real principle involved in Priscilla's counting on her fingers whenever she was called upon to work sums.

He was still pathetically concerned about the physical well-being of the children and spent hours devising inducements to get them into the open air. For example, he told Mary Grace and Priscilla that if they would go to a house a mile or so away, they would find an important letter addressed to them. So the two walked briskly to their destination and found there a note from their father: "Come home. You are good girls who have had a nice walk."[8]

Such tricks on Cooper's part irritated Priscilla, though they never alienated her affection. She grew up disliking exercise for its own sake, preferring an objective when she went roaming about the countryside—an orchard to rob or a deserted house to explore. There were many such houses in the neighborhood, relics of Bristol's past glory. In an undated letter to her brother, probably written in 1826, when she was about ten, she described an expedition to one of these desolate spots.

> The other day Mary, Juliana and I went to the deserted 'mansion of Peirce'. . . . After walking about the place, gathering together all the things left behind . . . which consisted of an old scrubbing brush, a tub without any bottom and a piece of paper, found in the temple of C—, I went to one of the back windows to see if I could not peep through it. When, to my

astonishment, it came open at my touch, I called to Mary and Juliana, and we lifted up the sash and saw a very comfortable room, a nice sofa, chairs with cushions on them, a table and a bunch of keys on it. Of course I could not withstand the temptation, and so I jumped in, sat down on each chair, lay down on the sofa, looked in two little closets, in which I found a leather shot bag and half a letter, which I secured. I then jumped out again, shut the window and went home, loaded with the scrubbing brush, bottomless tub, papers and the precious shot bag, which I wear, with the tub, suspended from my neck with a blue riband, not forgetting to mention a broken *pot de chambre*. . . . 'These are the ruins of the noblest man that ever lived in the tide of times.'[9]

Apparently Cooper's idea of putting happiness and health before books had begun to pay off in unexpected coin. The little girl who refused to master the rudiments of mathematics was developing a lively prose style. She was, moreover, reading with discrimination and appreciation. She quoted—to be true, with some inaccuracy—as if already she had a vested interest in Shakespeare—as indeed she had, for the great tragedies were her father's stock-in-trade, familiar to her as are the tools of the artisan to his child. She undertook at about this time to fill copy books with transcriptions of verse which appealed to her, and she and Mary Grace memorized what they liked best. When the family played the parlor game called "Capping Verses," it was nip and tuck between the elder sisters as to who would win. In this mild form of intellectual dissipation their mother often joined them, for Mary Fairlie Cooper had plenty of time to devote to her children and enjoyed taking part in their amusements and supplementing Miss Hannah's instruction with lessons in French and music, deemed essential for "accomplished" young women such as she hoped her girls would become.

Sometimes when Cooper was at home and there were no guests, the children would go over after their simple supper, served in the nursery, to have dessert with their parents, who dined elaborately. They were treated like adults and were encouraged to join in the conversation. Their father was a talented raconteur and exerted himself to please his small audience. One night he told them that Ludlow, an actor-manager friend of his, just back from the frontier, had sent a present to Priscilla. It seems that at Sandusky an Indian had ridden up, bearing before him on his pony a very small, very beautiful fawn. Ludlow had bought it as a present for his seven-year-old daughter; but when he took it to New York, the little creature had gnawed the furniture and broken the china. Cooper had taken it off his hands and brought it to Bristol, where it could enjoy greater freedom than in the city. The joyous excitement of his young listeners at the happy climax of this tale turned to sorrow the next day when the fawn leaped all the fences and made a shambles of the neighbors' gardens. Their mother, firm for once, said the little nuisance must go. Joseph Bonaparte, learning of the crisis, offered to take Priscilla's pet on his estate, where it would be well cared for. There it lived to become a handsome deer and was, many years afterward, taken to France when its new master returned to his own country.[10]

The loss of the fawn occasioned no noticeable gap in the long and interesting procession of pets that were treated as members of the family. The smallest puppy or the least of kittens was given a fine mouth-filling name and treated like a member of the family. Cooper was as bad as the children; he brought home two fighting cocks and insisted on keeping them in his own room until he found they crowed all night.[11] On one occasion when Julia Fairlie, the youngest of Mary's sisters, came to visit, she brought along twelve kittens and two cats in a basket on her lap, declaring that they had a "particular invitation" from their "Aunt Mary."[12]

Julia stayed for months at a time in Bristol, enjoying the relaxed tempo of the Cooper home. She was not so much older than Priscilla and Mary Grace that they felt in awe of her. However, there was considerable stiffening of the atmosphere when Major and Mrs. Fairlie and Aunt Louisa paid ceremonious visits in Bristol, as they did twice each year—usually during Cooper's absence. The family letters show that Mary Fairlie

Cooper's mother, Maria Fairlie, had drastic changes to suggest in her daughter's management of servants, houses, and garden and that her interference was not welcomed by the two older girls. Mary Grace wrote to her brother, Jim, in the summer of 1827, expressing some amusement at their grandmother's officious behavior during a recent visit:

We had the place all nicely cleaned up this year. But when Grandma came she began hoeing and weeding according to custom. And she really thinks she has arranged everything and that it was a perfect wilderness when she arrived. You know the four large clusters of sweetbriar in front of the house. She has tied the tops all together to make them look like arbors. You may imagine them.[13]

The fact that Priscilla called Mrs. Fairlie "the Duchess of Naut"[14] as soon as she was old enough to coin a phrase suggests that she resented any assumption of the superiority of the Cortlandt Street mansion to the Cooper home; yet being a lively and eager child, she could hardly have been indifferent to the delights of the metropolis when she and Mary Grace returned the visit and enjoyed with the Fairlies a touch of city life. Of all the joys a visit to New York afforded, attendance at the theatre gave her the most intoxicating pleasure. She lost no time on her return to Bristol in putting on versions of the plays she had seen. To this end she pressed into service her playmates and sisters, even the baby, Louisa. Since there was a shortage of boys willing to take part, she raided her brother's wardrobe in order that girls who enacted male roles might appear in style.

During one of Jim's absences, when Priscilla was about eleven, she wrote him the following letter, which, knowing her to be a tease, he would not have taken seriously, even if his mother had not written on the margin, "This is a lie. M. F. C."

We repeated our play on Thursday with unbounded applause. You can't think how well we all looked. Cordelia and Grace Riche had on two pairs of your transparencies, cut down, and jackets and waistcoats of yours, but as there was but one more jacket and that for me, the hero, poor Loo had to put up with an old cloth waistcoat, in which we put black silk sleeves. It, however, looked very so-so. I was dressed in a pair of your stripes, with red tape sewed down the seams, a waistcoat of yours, trimmed with red tape. The only difficulty we found was that when we took the red tape off for "The Four Mowbrays," which we intend soon to act, it left a red mark, which the united powers of Hannah Ward and Prissy Poor could not banish; so I was obliged to apply to Miss Hannah for another pair. By the by, Mary says you have a new coat. I wish you would send it by Grandpapa and Aunt Julia when they come. Mama intends writing to the gallant Tom to come up and bring his best coat with him, if you don't send on yours.[15]

During these early years Priscilla's artistic aspirations were not limited to the drama. She spent hours shut up in a summer-house at the foot of the garden, called by her "Celia's bower," and filled copy books with plays, poems, and stories of her own composition. One of these survives—an oblong brown volume (undated) called *Reflections of Celia.*[16] It is dedicated mysteriously "To the person I most love and esteem." Written on the fly leaf is a couplet which she attributes to Pope:

> Dear sacred name, rest ever unrevealed,
> Nor pass these lips in silence sealed.

The pretentious table of contents lists titles of many ambitious masterpieces she proposed to write but apparently never got around to. She copied verses from Shelley, Byron, Moore, and other favorites and included some pieces of her own—a little on the farcical side, such as "Celia Laments for Her Shift." There are ninety-one riddles, originated by the authoress, most of them as bad as Number 51.

> Question: Why is a drunkard like a man beating his wife?
> Answer: Because he is given to lick her.

This quaint relic of a childhood over a hundred years ago reflects the interests of a little girl with a gift for fun which must have made her irresistible to her brothers, her sisters, the young Meyers, Riches, and other members of "the crowd" that made 722 Radcliffe Street their rallying place.

Eighteen twenty-seven marks the end of an epoch in the history of Bristol. The Cooper family were doubtless present when on a fine summer day of that year a crowd assembled to celebrate the beginning of construction on a canal from Easton to Bristol. There was prayer at the Episcopal Church, a ceremonial first shovelful of dirt put in a wheelbarrow, a speech, and cheers and singing. Sixty miles long with twenty-four locks, costing over $1,000,000, this project, not completed until 1832, waked the community from its lethargy.[17] And when the rumor of a railroad's being built became a reality, as it shortly did, no one could say that Bristol was "the world forgetting by the world forgot."

Seeing so much bustle about them, the Coopers probably assumed the right to share in the prosperity of which these events seemed a prelude. Lulled into a false sense of security, they seemed singularly unaware of signs and portents of disaster which less happy people would have recognized as such. Cooper at this time fell short of the 4,500 nights of performance Hornblow lists as his accomplishment by 1830,[18] but his exertion had been sufficient to cause his magnificent strength to wane.[19] Of late when he returned from a tour he was weary—a thing unheard of in the heyday of his career. He was inclined to minimize the importance of the fact that although he was still extravagantly admired in the provincial theatres, in the larger cities there was lately a noticeable falling off in the enthusiasm of his audiences.[20] Having been for so long successful and prosperous, he optimistically supposed that time would remedy the indifference of the public and that rest and change would better his health. He determined to go to England that year—not, however, until he had seen his son, James, settled at Christ's Church School at Cowneck, where Mr. Clark prepared boys for the examinations at West Point.

It had been decided that Jim was to follow in his grandfather's, Major Fairlie's, footsteps and become a soldier. His departure and that of his father in the fall of 1827 left a gap in the family circle, which his mother and his sisters tried to fill by inviting

MAJOR JAMES FAIRLIE

BY THOMAS SULLY

MARIA YATES FAIRLIE

BY THOMAS SULLY

Julia Fairlie, the girls' young aunt, to come for a visit. But not even her presence could enliven a monotony which, as Mary described it to her absent son, sounds like something from one of Jane Austen's novels:

> You know Bristol is very dull at this season, and if you wish anything like news from us it must be manufactured. Yet though I confess that our life here is very dull from want of society, it has its charms and comforts too. Our house is very snug and warm; we have good servants; good though plain dinners; cakes of all kinds in abundance; and the country luxuries of apples and nuts in lots. With the exception of Charles, it is an entirely female establishment, though far from a nunnery in its habits.
>
> The mornings are passed by the girls and Miss W. in school, and your Aunt Julia and I read or write or sew, most usually in my chamber. After dinner if the weather will allow, they all take a walk (except me) or a romp—If kept within doors, some romping or playing is sure to go on. We assemble in the parlor as soon [as] or before dark, and then commences the ball. With Virginia and your Aunt Julia a complete cotillion is formed and I strum for them till Charles brings tea.
>
> After tea if we have no company the girls get their . . . work, the little ones pencil and paper or perhaps . . . I am the reader. We have read several of Walter Scott's novels and some better books Sundays. If they can't go to evening church I read them a couple of sermons. So here you have 'our day.' . . . To my stupid tastes, a very comfortable life, for no discord or misery intrudes; and though nothing very exquisitely delightful occurs, yet nothing very unpleasant interrupts the 'even tenor of our way.'[21]

The serenity of Mary Fairlie Cooper's spirit must have been considerably disturbed when, on her husband's return from England in 1828, he entered into a disastrous venture with Ludlow. The two men leased the Chatham Theatre in New York, and Cooper undertook to attract audiences there in competition to young Edwin Forrest, who nightly packed the Second Bowery Theatre. For ten performances the veteran actor met with reasonable success, but at the end of that time he departed quite suddenly, leaving Ludlow to struggle with the debts incurred and to feel that he had been treated shabbily.[22] The sobering realization that Cooper, now fifty-two years of age, had passed the zenith of his popularity was becoming inescapable, and the problem of the education of the children, especially of Jim, began to weigh heavily upon the whole family.[23] Priscilla, her brother's favorite among his sisters, was old enough at fifteen to await anxiously answers to letters her mother addressed to her old friend, Martin Van Buren, adviser to President Jackson, and to feel—just as Cooper was about to see "Old Hickory" himself—a great tide of relief at the news that Jim's appointment to West Point had gone through. When a letter a few days later from her Aunt Louisa Fairlie announced that James had passed the examinations, Priscilla and Mary Grace wept. Their father told Jim so in a heavily paternal letter of congratulations, dated July 13, 1830.

Your mother and Mary and Priscilla were found crying over your Aunt Louisa's letter above mentioned. They were tears of pleasure. How deep the mortification, how bitter the feelings that would accrue should [news] of a different nature ever reach their ears. But that I will not for a moment think possible. You must feel too much gratification yourself to run the risk of losing the 'mens sibi conscia recte' by carelessness, inattention or mad conduct. But this ought to be sufficient. *Aut Caesar, aut nihil.*

Your mother writes me word that you wish to have a writing desk. My writing desk has been newly repaired and fitted up. You may write home to have it sent to you by any favorable opportunity. I am not sure where the key is. If not in the lock, it most likely is in the drawer on the right in my bureau or perhaps in one of the pigeon holes.[24]

Mary Fairlie Cooper's letter on this occasion was filled with anxiety and maternal concern that Cadet James Fairlie Cooper take full advantage of this heaven-sent opportunity to prepare himself for a career less hazardous than his father's.

Remember, my dear son, the present time makes or mars your character forever. . . . Your father has no fortune to give you. Your own exertion must be your means of living. And what profession is there half so good as the one your present situation and studies tend to. The law, physics, divinity are overstocked with starving aspirants. To be a merchant there must be capital. The stage I trust you have never thought of. Your father's example would deter you from that, and yet how few actors have ever arrived at the height and respectability he has attained. But pleasing a capricious public taste must be the worst form of slavery. It is a profession that depends upon the slightest accident to be destroyed. I could write a volume upon this point, but I am sure it is unnecessary.[25]

The reaction of the more youthful members of the family, Mary Grace and Priscilla, was partly elation at Jim's good fortune and partly delighted realization that through him they could now meet any number of handsome youths dressed in becoming uniforms. As soon as Jim was settled, Mary took the girls and their pretty aunt, Julia Fairlie, to The Point, and from that time on the letters that passed between his sisters and Jim were full of inquiries and information about the young men they had met there. Priscilla wrote in the spring of 1831:

I am very glad you intend introducing Stockton to us, as I was more pleased with him and Scot than any of the cadets. We have a very good opportunity of discovering who is the best of the cadets by a book that Papa purchased last winter. We are astonished to find that Scot has no marks whatsoever against him, but Stockton has 42. Our friend Roy Dix was found deficient and sent back to 4th class and has 1040 something—I forgot what.[26]

The Cooper girls were growing up and beginning to take an interest in beaux and clothes. They were not quite ready for conquests themselves, but with the fascinated interest of amateurs taking notes on the technique of an expert, they observed Julia Fairlie play fast and loose with the hearts of men. Two years before they had been amused and slightly superior about a flirtation she had conducted in Bristol with an impressionable young man, Mr. George. Mary Grace had written to Jim, then at Cowneck, a satirical account of the affair:

Julia is dying in love with Mr. George and he is with her. He comes here very often. He says she is 'the essence of his soul' and a great number of such extravagant phrases. However, Mr. George fainted the other night, and fell down on our sofa when we told him Mademoiselle Celeste was married to some Mr. Elliot. You know Mr. George is desperately in love with her.[27]

Before the visit to West Point such behavior on the part of adults had apparently seemed to them silly; but their attitude toward Julia's romance with Mr. Park, one of Jim's older friends at the Academy whom they met on his visit in 1830, was that of confidantes eager for every scrap of information. They were delighted when Julia sent her lover her miniature,[28] and must have been greatly disappointed when the heroine of the affair grew indifferent and went to the Springs, troubled by nothing more serious than a desire to spread her conquests further.

Stay-at-homes themselves, Priscilla and Mary Grace read eagerly Julia's accounts of her adventures at Balston, where she went to see and be seen.

Can you believe it possible that I was fifteen days at the Springs, in the midst of the gayety and fashion of New York with *three* frocks—a shabby black silk for the morning, and for dinner another black silk and a grey one? How do you think I managed? Why, first I wore the grey, and then by way of variety, the grey with white gigots; the next day black, then black with white sleeves until I had gone the rounds.

I suppose you think I looked like a cat in a strange garret. No such thing! I got along very well, danced every night, played billiards every morning, and talked (!) a little.[29]

Frivolity was hard to achieve in Bristol, but Priscilla and Mary Grace took advantage of every opportunity. When Captain Childs brought the Washington Greys from Philadelphia for an encampment in celebration of the Fourth of July, 1830, Mary Fairlie Cooper thought the girls old enough to take part in the festivities. She wrote to Jim about how the soldiers serenaded the town the first night and how the next morning his sisters visited the camp in the Pines, where everything was "*a la militaire.*" The troops drilled and fired the cannon. Afterwards the entire company was invited to a public dinner. Mary Grace and Priscilla, so their mother reports, danced a cotillion, "all Bristol staring in the bright sunlight of noontide."[80]

The Cooper letters in the summer of 1830 are gay and full of the idle persiflage affected by fashionable people of the period. Until the fall of that year no shadow fell across the pages of the news the family wrote to Jim at West Point and to the Fairlies in New York. Suddenly and unexpectedly grief and responsibility brought an end to the carefree girlhoods of Priscilla and Mary Grace and forced them into an abrupt maturity. Their first realization of the finality of death came in October, when Major Fairlie died, old and full of honors. This tragedy occurred at a time when their mother, expecting the birth of a child, was scarcely well enough to stand the strain of the large and impressive funeral accorded her father. He was buried with military honors; and the Society of the Cincinnati, the members of the bar, and the most distinguished citizens in New York followed the funeral train. This was death and burial at its dignified best; and the elder Cooper girls, who rode in the carriage with their mother, found in the occasion nothing to shock and dismay them as did the birth and death of their little brother, Stephen Decatur, which followed almost immediately.

Mary Fairlie Cooper made a slow recovery after these disasters and leaned heavily upon Mary Grace and Priscilla; they shared her pain and grief as they nursed her through a period of depression and of failing health which was the prologue to her last illness. An elegiac tone pervaded a long letter which Mary Fairlie Cooper wrote in October, 1830, to her old friend, Washington Irving, now a gay bachelor living abroad. It did not sound like the letters "the fascinating Fairlie" wrote to him in the days when she was the belle of New York. Although she did not mention her troubles and told him very simply about the deaths of her father and of her infant son, an autumnal melancholy pervaded her comments on the news she gave of old friends. Only when she wrote of her children did she exemplify her accustomed charm and good spirits.

My eldest daughter is no beauty, but she is everything else a parent's heart could wish—temper, mind, disposition: perfect; understanding: excellent. And with very little instruction, and in some branches, entirely self-taught. Her younger sisters—at least three of them—are entirely instructed by her.

My next child, my only son, James Fairlie Cooper, is a cadet at West Point—and a noble youth he is—and stands very high there already, although only entered there last June.

My next, Priscilla, is the genius (there must be a genius in the family). She is just past fourteen, but as tall as I am. She is all talent—that is, in regard to sprightliness of mind, cleverness in writing, and fun and drollery in everything; but so incapable of application that she has not of what is technically called accomplishments a single one. She is the editress of a family newspaper which is in great demand wherever a number has been seen. She is not beautiful, but there is something very piquant in her countenance . . .

My four remaining girls are, of course, all children and though very dear to their parents, cannot hope to excite much interest elsewhere. I have only one decided beauty in the whole six Misses Cooper. She has a beauty's name too: Olivia. She is lovely indeed—a perfect little heroine, lovely in mind as in feature.[31]

This letter is one of the few documents among the Cooper Papers from 1830 to 1833. A journal kept by Mary Grace begins in November, 1831, with a fragmentary account of a Southern tour with her father; but someone has ruthlessly cut from the little book the pages dealing with the next two years, which witnessed the invalidism of Mary Fairlie Cooper and the failing fortunes of her husband. It is quite possible that Mary Grace herself destroyed the record of a period she wished never to remember, and it is perhaps not an accident that no family letters survive dealing with the anxieties and sorrow of the family at this time.

Fortunately there are two letters from Washington Irving, newly returned from triumphs abroad, to bridge the gap in family chronicles. He wrote on June 21, 1832, from Philadelphia to his brother, Peter, still in Paris, giving him news of their old friend, Tom Cooper, and his family.

This morning I was seated at breakfast at the public table of the Mansion House, when Cooper entered to take his repast. I recognized him instantly; indeed, he retains much of his shape and look, though the former is a little squarer and heavier. I immediately accosted him. He took his seat beside me, and we had an interesting dish of chat.

He was on the point of starting for his home at Bristol, and invited me to pay his wife and family a visit, and return in the afternoon steam boat. So said, so done. I took my seat beside him in a light, open carriage, with a tall stripling in the uniform of a cadet of West Point, whom he introduced as his eldest son, and who had much of his mother's countenance.

I found Mary Fairlie in a pretty cottage in the pretty town of Bristol, on the banks of the Delaware. She was pale and thinner than I had expected to find her, yet still retaining much of her former self. I passed a very agreeable and interesting day there. . . .

After dinner with them, I got on board a steam boat that was passing at five o'clock, and was whisked up to the city in an hour and a half.[32]

On Irving's return to America he was inclined to be pleased with everything and everybody he saw. He seems to have viewed the Coopers through rose-colored glasses—or perhaps he was too kind a gentleman to let himself see what they would not have wished him to know: that Mary was far from well and the family in straitened circumstances. A few days later he wrote to Peter again—this time more realistically.

New York
June 28, 1832

Since writing the foregoing I saw Cooper act a few scenes from *Macbeth* before a very thin Philadelphia audience. He acted much as formerly, excepting rather more slowly and heavily. His form is still fine on the stage but his countenance is muzzy and indistinct. I was engaged for the evening and could stay only to the end of his dagger and murder scene. I should think his Macbeth equal to any they have at present in England, though this is not saying much.

It did not relish with me, however, as in the olden time; but a thin and cold-hearted audience is enough to dampen the spirit of a performer, and to chill the feelings of a spectator.[33]

It is just as well that Irving wrote so casually of the Coopers and that Mary Grace's record of 1832-1833 was destroyed. It would be painful to read of the slow decline of Mary Fairlie Cooper after the birth and death of another little son, who survived just long enough to be christened William Gaston. She did not live to see her husband completely crowded off the stage by the American actors, Forrest and Payne, and the English stars, the Kembles, Tyrone Power, and the Keans. She died after a long and painful illness on March 19, 1833, aged forty-three. If she had lived to experience the financial disaster that overtook the family after her death, she would have been proud to see the united front with which they faced the world and the loyalty with which Priscilla and Mary Grace rallied to help their father protect the little sisters from any sense of insecurity.

3

THE CURTAIN RISES

1833-1834

After Mary Fairlie Cooper's death Maria Fairlie took it for granted that her daughter's children were now hers. In a letter written March 5, 1834, to her sister-in-law, Mrs. Yates, she expressed a melancholy satisfaction in that fact:

I have been torn by conflicting circumstances to a state of pitiable weakness, not the least is the idea of again becoming a wanderer and breaking up housekeeping in May for Bristol. The graves of my children call me, and the dear living ones will be alone. . . .

In the same letter another passage indicates how strong was her prejudice against her actor son-in-law.

I ought to mention that what has been appropriated for the children of Mr. Cooper has been so completely tied up from the father that he in no way whatever can claim any part of it, not even the interest.[1]

There is plenty of evidence in Mary Grace's diary that Mrs. Fairlie was a difficult old lady. The entry of August 28, 1835, for example, gave a long account of her disinheriting her daughter Julia, who entertained Ralph Lockwood, a caller of whom she disapproved.

How horribly . . . Grand-ma must treat poor Julia about Lockwood. . . . She has actually written a will, which she brought downstairs for John to sign as witness, something to this effect:

"I, Maria Fairlie, being strong in mind though weak in body, do bequeath all my property to my daughter Julia, with this proviso: that she does not marry that loafer, Lockwood, in which case I leave all I possess to my son John, on condition that if Julia marries the detested Ralph, he does not give her any portrait of her father or myself or any of my family or anything that has belonged to her family by her disgraced. In case of their death or noncompliance to my injunctions I bequeath everything to my beloved grandchild, Olivia Perry Cooper." (John got a fit of laughter.) This was stuck over by several seals of black wax.

She walks out of the room when Lockwood comes, so that John has told him not to come any more. She talks about red noses constantly before him and insults him in every way. Julia says she has refused him, but if she is persecuted in this way she does not know what may be the consequences.[2]

Elsewhere are references to quarrels with her eldest son, John, who sometimes amused himself in the morning by giving her "a little filial blowing up."[3]

Cooper, realizing that Maria Fairlie would be a discordant element in the household, may be forgiven for declining her help, and preferring, for a time at least, to get on as best he could with the help of the older girls and the faithful servant, appropriately named Susan Poor. In spite of the reasonableness of his stand, in the family quarrel which followed her mother's death in 1833 Mary Grace suffered a conflict of loyalties which she records in her journal:

I cannot forgive Papa for his selfishness (for there is no other name for his feeling) on this occasion. And when I reflect on Grandmama's age and our prospects of travelling continually so that we may never have the opportunity of being together again, it cuts me to the heart.[4]

That Priscilla, as always, stood staunchly by her father may be inferred from a passage in a letter written to Mary Grace in 1837, when the elder sister was visiting in South Carolina:

Mrs. Royal Highness of Naut [her grandmother] is coming today, and I shall want your gentle influence to make her behave herself, for I fear that she and I will have a tremendous fight. Whenever she interferes, my blood boils in my body and I have to bite my tongue to prevent myself from being impertinent to her. I shan't try to prevent myself any longer if she doesn't come more amiable than when she went.[5]

Cooper had problems more vital to him than a disapproving mother-in-law. For five or six years, as his professional earnings had grown less, the demands of his growing family had increased. Always he had spent his large but uncertain income and his splendid energy with profligate disregard for the future. Like the hero of a great tragedy, cursed by what Aristotle called "a tragic fault," he had moved towards inevitable catastrophe. He now faced the realization of failing physical strength and of his inability to do what he wished for his children. The future of James, in his third year at West Point, was provided for; but that of the six Misses Cooper, especially the four youngest, was a matter of real concern.

After their mother's death Priscilla and Mary Grace encouraged him in such self-deception as placing the responsibility for his predicament upon hard times rather than upon his own improvidence. In 1833 everyone short of funds was blaming Jackson's ill-advised removal of the public money from the Bank of the United States for falling stocks, bankruptcies, the high rate of interest on loans.[6]

The sun of prosperity shone on few, and clouds hung low and threatening over those who made their living in the theatre. Ireland states that "a certain indifference to any but newcomers marked this period of dramatic history, and unless absolute novelty, either in play or performer was announced, the finest combination that America could produce sufficed but little in the way of attraction, even with the most approved productions found in dramatic literature."[7] The managers with whom Cooper had worked for years suddenly were interested only in such good risks as young Payne or Forrest, or such foreign stars as the Kembles; they did not wish to engage an aging actor whose parts were all too familiar to the public. They were not, however, unmindful of Cooper's long years of faithful service. Although he had held himself aloof from his fellows and had been, to tell the truth, proud and arrogant at times, he had warm friends and admirers, who, seeing him deeply troubled, busied themselves to relieve his immediate needs. They planned a series of complimentary benefits to create what was called "The Cooper Fund."

There is little probability that Mary Grace and Priscilla attended the first of these entertainments, for it took place in Philadelphia, June, 1833, only three months after their mother's death. The distinguished English stars, Charles Kemble and his daughter, Fanny, volunteered their services to play Jaffier and Belvidera to the Pierre of Cooper in *Venice Preserved;* Mr. Rice sang on the festive occasion his popular Negro song, "Jim Crow." The box office took in considerably more than $2,500.

An equally distinguished cast—Hamblin, Wallack, and Josephine Clifton—contributed their services for the New York benefit, which followed on November 7, 1833. Samuel Woodworth, famous poetaster of his day, the author of "The Old Oaken Bucket," wrote an elegant address which was delivered by Mr. Hamblin:

> The King comes here tonight. He who could wring
> Our hearts at will was 'every inch a king'! . . .
> The drama was his empire; and his throne
> No rival dared dispute—he reigned alone!

For almost a hundred lines the eulogy continued, skillfully weaving into riming couplets mention of twenty-six of the 116 parts Ireland gives as comprising Cooper's repertoire.[8] At the conclusion of this fulsome introduction, as Hamblin delivered the lines, "He was and *is* 'in every inch a King,'" Cooper was presented to the audience. He was so overcome by the honor paid him and by the tumult of applause with which he was greeted that he had difficulty in reciting "Alexander's Feast," his contribution to the evening's entertainment.

Financially, as well as in personal satisfaction, it was a most successful benefit; he was richer by $4,500. He expressed his gratitude to the friends who organized the project, the actors who contributed their services, to the press and to those who had come to the performance in a fine, dignified letter, published in the New York papers.[9] It was expected that he would now retire gracefully, with the applause of his friends ringing in his ears. He should have known how to make a dramatic exit, and doubtless did, but necessity overruled his sense of the fitness of things. A prudent man who had been in Cooper's shoes might have died rich. Tyrone Power had recently made £7,000 on one American tour; and Matthews, $11,000.[10] Tom Cooper had formerly commanded fees comparable to theirs. He had thrown away enough on luxury and the gaming table to have made him comfortable for life.

The $7,000 the two benefits had earned must have seemed to such a spendthrift an insignificant sum, sufficient to furnish pocket money but not a real solution to his problem. He felt sure there was a better way out of the present difficulties than an appeal to the generosity of his friends. He talked the matter over with his two elder girls, who had become his partners in the effort to care for the family. In one of their discussions about money Priscilla told him she had promised her mother that if it were necessary she would go upon the stage.[11] Such an idea was shocking to Cooper, who had protected his children from all contact with his theatrical life.

It is impossible to know what changed his opinion. Perhaps he found in the recent phenomenal success of the Kembles, father and daughter, precedent for the Coopers to follow their example. The fact that Fanny Kemble had lost neither social position nor reputation but was eagerly sought out by all the leading people may have led him to realize that a young woman like Priscilla would escape censure if she were carefully guarded from the unsavory aspects of life back-stage. Whatever influenced his decision, the fact is that soon he began to coach her during the weary months of his enforced idleness. She must have been an apt pupil; before the members of the family in New York were aware of his plan, the arrangements were completed for her appearance there February 17, 1834, at the Bowery Theatre, in the role of Virginia in Sheridan Knowles's tragedy, *Virginius.* His intention was kept secret, for it was not difficult to foresee the reaction of the Fairlies, socially sensitive to the slightest change in the varying wind of public opinion.

Her father had a sentimental preference that Priscilla's first performance take place at the Park, with which he had been formerly closely associated; but the manager, Mr. Simpson, was uncooperative and the Bowery Theatre proved more hospitable. The press was kind. There was a great deal of publicity before the performance, the article in the New York *Post* on the morning of the fateful day being typically sympathetic:

The Evening Post, Monday, February 17, 1834.

Mr. Cooper, the veteran tragedian of the American stage, takes his benefit this evening in the Bowery Theatre, and gives great additional interest to the occasion by using it to introduce his daughter to the stage. The play of *Virginius* is chosen for the purpose, the father sustaining the part of the heroic old centurion and the daughter that of his interesting and persecuted child. Their actual relationship thus corresponding with that of their assumed characters will cause the scene to be looked upon with more unmindful pleasure than when Mr. Kemble acts the gay suitor to his daughter and when they bandy between them with full emphasis and point, some of the not very delicate allusions and repartee of Benedict and Beatrice. The daughter of Mr. Cooper, we understand, possesses talents which justify the anticipation that she will, with the requisite experience, make an excellent actress. Her attempt this evening will of course be viewed with the greatest lenity and kindness; for the situation of a young and diffident girl, appearing for the first time before a crowded audience, must be conceived to be highly embarrassing. The Virginius of Mr. Cooper was in former days a notable piece of acting and we hope to see it so sustained tonight that no one will have reason to say, "Superfluous lags the veteran on the stage."

The entertainment offered by Mr. Cooper for his benefit in addition to the attraction of his own name and that of his daughter, presents also the inducement of Mr. Forrest in Den-

AMERICAN

THEATRE....BOWERY.

MR. COOPER'S

Benefit and Last Appearance,

On which occasion he begs to announce, to his Friends and the Public, that his Daughter,

MISS P. E. COOPER,

Will make her First Appearance on any Stage, in the character of

VIRGINIA.

Mr. Cooper as Virginius

And for this occasion only, the following gentlemen have kindly volunteered their services—

Mr. Forrest, as Dentatus,
Mr. Hamblin, as Icilius,
Mr. Wallack, as Mr. Somerton.

On Monday Evening, February 17th, 1834,

Will be acted, the Tragedy of

Virginius

Virginius,............................ Mr. Cooper
Dentatus,............................Mr. Forrest
Icilius,..............................Mr. Hamblin

Appius Claudius,.....Mr. Gale	Cracius,..........Mr. Addis
Caius Claudius,........Collins	Marius,.............Hanson
Numitorius, ...McClure	Lucius,.............Wheatley
Titus,...............Marble	Oppius,.............Baldock
Servius,..............Lewis	Soldiers, Citizens, Lictors, &c.

Virginia,...............by......Miss P. E. Cooper

Servia,........Mrs. Stevenson	Slave,......................

To conclude with the Farce of My

Neighbour's Wife.

Mr. Somerton,..................... Mr. Wallack

Timothy Brown,...Mr. Flynn	Mrs. Somerton,....Mrs. Flynn
Jonathan Smith.........Gates	Mrs. Brown,.....Mrs. Herring

Mrs. Smith,.............................Mrs. Stevenson

☞ON WEDNESDAY EVENING, FEBRUARY 19th, 1834,

Mr. Forrest's Benefit

A New and Splendid Melo-dramatic Spectacle, called

The Maid of the Mist:

Or Ann of Glerstein.

With new Scenery, Dresses, & Decorations has been some time in preparation, and will be produced in a few days.

J. W. BELL PRINTER, 17 ANN-STREET.

tatus and Mr. Hamblin in Icilius. We copy the following paragraph from the *Mercantile Advertizer* (Feb. 15, 1834):

"On Monday night Mr. Cooper takes a benefit at the American Theatre, Bowery, and will on that occasion bring out his daughter, Miss E. P. Cooper, in the character of Virginia. It has been whispered about for several months that Mr. Cooper was instructing her for the stage and we learn that great interest is felt for the success of this fair *debutante*. Report speaks very favorably of this young lady, and the numerous friends of her family will doubtless give her a cheering welcome. The tragedy is to be strongly cast—thus, Virginius, Mr. Cooper; Dentatus, Mr. Forrest; Icilius, Mr. Hamblin."

We take pleasure in mentioning another instance among many of that kindness and liberality on the part of Mr. Forrest, which have won for him golden opinions from all sorts of people. As soon as he heard that the manager with his usual liberality had decided to give Mr. Cooper a benefit, Mr. Forrest offered his services; the beneficiary asked him to play the part of Virginius, to which he immediately assented. Yesterday it was hinted to him that Miss Cooper on her debut would feel more confidence if her father played that part. Mr. Forrest consented in a moment to take the part of Dentatus. The public we trust will fully appreciate Mr. Forrest's motives and award to him that mead of praise which such an act merits.[12]

This preview which, though flattering, has the Coopers sharing the limelight with Forrest, was followed the day after the performance, February 18, 1834, by a briefer but no less kindly article:

The Bowery Theatre was crowded last evening and a feeling of the utmost kindness was manifested towards the diffident maiden of whose first public effort they were to be the judges. No female possessing that degree of sensitiveness and modesty which is the invariable accompaniment of genius ever made a very successful first appearance. Those who succeed very well at first are not apt to continue successful long. To what degree of excellence Miss Cooper, with study and practice, may rise, it is impossible to predict. Those who have had the best opportunities of observing her talent, speak in high terms of it.

One scene last evening was particularly affecting—it was that in which Virginius describes what a treasure his daughter had

THOMAS A. COOPER AS HAMLET

BY THOMAS SULLY

MARY FAIRLIE COOPER

BY WILLIAM DUNLAP

been to him since his wife's death—how she had been his 'sweet companion, pupil, tutor, child,' and with what anxious and mingled feelings he had watched over her education. The perfect and touching applicability of the language to the real circumstances of this widowed tragedian and his motherless girl drew tears from many an eye.[13]

In regard to her talent there were dissenting voices, but no one then or since has questioned the purity of her motives. "Connected through her mother with several distinguished New York families, the refined and charming girl essayed the boards merely to prop the failing fortunes of her father,"[14] says Odell in *Annals of the New York Stage.* Mr. Ireland echoes this opinion:

The devotion to her family which induced this young lady to enter a profession repugnant to her disposition was fully appreciated by her many friends, who gave her on this occasion all the encouragement that their presence and applause could bestow; while her interesting appearance, girlish, graceful manners, her sunny countenance, shaded by clustering curls of golden hair, and the real merit she displayed, awakened all the kindlier feelings of the most indifferent portion of the audience, so that the difficult path she has been forced to tread promises to be not wholly free from gleams of sunshine and satisfaction.[15]

The dramatic fitness of the father and daughter upon the stage being in real life father and daughter escaped no one. Years later Anna Cora Ogden (Mrs. Mowatt) borrowed the incident for her story, "Stella."[16] There she describes how, when the lovely girl, the symbol of filial devotion, stepped from the wings, the audience was moved to tears by her first speech: "Well, Father, what is your wish?"

This sympathetic reaction was something of a triumph, for the distinguished people present that night had come to countenance but not to approve the appearance on the stage of one of the first girls, born and bred a lady, who ever defied the prejudice against the theatre as a profession for women. From the cloistered seclusion of her home in Bristol, Priscilla Cooper stepped into the glare of the footlights—a dutiful daughter—no more, no less. A kind of selflessness dignified her unconventional conduct. She was not to be mistaken by the most censorious for a stage-struck adolescent. By her youth and defenselessness she disarmed criticism, even that of her brother, Jim, who was shocked, as very young men usually are, by anything out of the ordinary in the conduct of their sisters. Immediately after her debut on February 17, 1834, she wrote to him:

I know, my dear brother, that I should have written to you before in regard to the step I have taken, but both my mind and body have been in such a commotion that I found it impossible; so I let you learn from others what I ought to have told you myself. I hoped, my dearest brother, to have received a letter from you encouraging me and approving of my endeavor to assist Papa. Such a letter would have been a very great comfort to me—a very great support in all my trials; and I feel sure you would have written if you could with truth have done so. When you know it was our dear Mother's desire that I should go upon the stage I am sure you will think me right. She often talked to me about it and encouraged me in it. If it were not for that one sustaining reflection I never could support the many dangers and disagreeable [circumstances] attending the life before me. You will be pleased to hear I have received the kindest and most affectionate letters from Mrs. B.—, and Mrs. — has also written me most warmly indeed. The encouraging commendations of all my friends reconciles me to almost anything. Papa looks so much happier and everything so much brighter that I am sure I am right in having waived all merely personal considerations in this matter.[17]

During the following months a legend gained credence in theatrical circles, to the effect that public life was so repugnant to her she fainted after every performance. This romantic fiction attributes to her more sensibility and less common sense than she possessed. Mary Grace's journal and Priscilla's letters indicate that she enjoyed the first year or two as her father's leading lady. Protected by him and cared for by her elder sister, she was quite happy when houses were good and her papa seemed cheerful. She took a normal amount of interest in clothes, beaux, and parties. Her head was not turned by flattery or applause, although she relished both. Her judgment was sound in regard to the young men who made respectful love to her. In her letter to Jim, written after the ovation accorded her first performance, she seems to be what she was from first to last, a well-balanced young woman, happily lacking in what is called "temperament."

You have seen by the papers accounts of my success. Papa's difficulty with Simpson[18] forced me to appear at the Bowery, but the crowd that was assembled there to sustain me was composed of the best people in New York. They all called on me, and I received flowers and messages and notes from all quarters.

But all this did not prevent my being frightened nearly out of my senses. I cannot describe it all; it was like a dreadful dream from the time my hair was dressed until I got back safely to my room at the hotel. A great many of Mamma's old friends called on me, the Hosacks,[19] Mrs. Paulding,[20] Mrs. Lawrence,[21] and many, many others, with most familiar names. Francis and Dr. Hosack both came to see me, and the day after the play Dr. Hosack sent me the kindest and most complimentary newspaper. . . .[22]

Just as would be expected, Maria Fairlie said and did the wrong thing. Not only was her disapproval of her granddaughter's choice of a profession outspoken, but apparently she failed to live up to the ideal she had of herself as never failing in hospitality. There is something pathetic in the humble confession of error she makes to Mrs. Yates in a letter, dated March 5, 1834, after the Coopers had left New York:

At this moment I feel severely the various ills flesh is heir to. My besetting sin, worldly pride, has been wounded a few days since, for I was totally unprepared for Priscilla Cooper's appearance on the stage. The dear child's reception by our family was unkind. It induced her father to take her to a boarding house.[23]

Priscilla forgave her after a fashion. Subsequent entries in Mary Grace's journal record dutiful visits paid to the Fairlies. "Persuaded Priss to call on Grandmama." "Priss happy to find no one at Grandmama's."

With the New York performance behind them, they went to Philadelphia, where they presented *Virginius* again on the twenty-eighth of March, 1834. Forrest was not in the cast on this occasion. Whatever he did or said was newsworthy, but Cooper was an actor out of favor with the public, so his presence and that of his daughter occasioned no comment in the press. Relieved that they were through with their engagements before critical Eastern audiences, who inevitably compared Priscilla to the more experienced Fanny Kemble, the Coopers turned their faces South, where they were sure of a welcome. Mary Grace accompanied them as wardrobe mistress and as chaperone for seventeen-year-old Priscilla.

They went by the route Tom Cooper usually took,[24] through Virginia to Columbia, South Carolina, and then to Charleston. There they followed such attractions as Tyrone Power, Jim Crow Rice, and Zip Coon at the Queen Street Theatre—a wretched place, better suited for a circus than for the performance of plays. The papers pronounced their engagement a success, stating that when "old actor-gentleman" Cooper and his "accomplished" Priscilla took their bows, there was so much applause that it fairly shook the frame building.[25]

In Charleston no one of Cooper's following was more enthusiastic than J. B. Irving, a veteran theatre-goer. He thought the performance magnificent but protested, as he always did, against the scene in which Virginius stabs Virginia, his daughter, with his sword. "No one with arms was permitted on the Forum," he insisted. As he sat in the audience that night he consoled himself for violation of historical accuracy by his delight in the stage pictures achieved by the grace and beauty of the actors; these he declared "fit for the study of a painter."[26]

Priscilla tried out in two new parts before the friendly Southerners: Beatrice to her father's Benedict and Juliet to his Romeo.[27]

Long in advance of the occasion, the Louisiana *Advertiser* carried notices of the "Grand Dramatic Festival for the Benefit of T. A. Cooper and His Children," which Edwin Forrest was promoting in New Orleans. It was to take place on April 14, at the American Theatre.

On April 2 the paper carried this announcement:

It will be seen by a notice below, signed by our most respectable citizens that a call for a meeting is made, to be held tomorrow evening, at half past seven o'clock, in Bishop's dining room, for the purpose of making arrangements for a benefit to the veteran tragedian Cooper, after the manner of those given him in Philadelphia and New York.

The money produced by these benefits are [sic] by deeds of trust paid over to certain trustees, to be by them invested in stocks. The income arising therefrom, so far as necessary, and so long as it shall be needed, to be applied to the education of the six daughters of Mr. Cooper. After the death of the father, the trust money to be divided among the daughters or the survivors of them, free from the control of their husbands should they marry.

We trust, for the credit of our city, that the meeting will be numerously attended. The friends of the drama particularly should not fail to be present to testify their sense of the high estimation in which we know they have ever held the veteran Father of the American Stage, who for thirty-eight years has delighted those who have witnessed his masterly presental of the heroes of the immortal Shakespeare.[28]

Notice of the arrival of the Coopers appeared on April 12; lists of committees, of actors who had volunteered their services for the program had been given in every issue for a week before. The bill was designed to please a wide variety of tastes.

THE AMERICAN THEATRE
APRIL 14, 1834

Desdemona — Mrs. Rowe

After which the interesting Drama of the *Hunter of the Alps*

Felix de Rosalvi — Mr. Caldwell
Jeronymo — Allen

At the end of the Drama a Grand Musical Olio

"The Dashing White Sergeant," by Mrs. Knight
"The Lass wi' the bonnie blu E'en," by Mr. Sinclair

After which the fourth act of *Virginius*

Virginius — Mr. Cooper
Virginia — Miss Cooper

The evening's entertainment to conclude with the admirable Petit Comedy of the *Dumb Bells*.[29]

Forrest did not act that night, but it was announced that he would delay his proposed trip abroad long enough to play Dentatus to Priscilla's Virginia at a later date.

On the morning of the performance, April 14, 1834, the *Advertiser* gave space for more publicity:

The Cooper Benefit—This grand dramatic festival is to be given tonight and promises to be a most splendid affair. The boxes and seats are almost already taken and we doubt not the house will be well crowded. All the artists of distinction in the city and its vicinity have with a laudable generosity tendered their services and the selections for the entertainment have been made as judiciously as possible.

It is not necessary for us to enter into any details in regard to the services rendered by Mr. Cooper in raising the legitimate drama in this country to its present high rank. He came to America nearly forty years ago and has ever since remained firm and consistent in his love to the country of his early adoption. He from the commencement of his arrival amongst us, identified himself with our feelings and interests.

Similar benefits have been given to Mr. Cooper in the cities of Philadelphia and New York, and for the credit of our city we are anxious that on this occasion New Orleans should not be behind her sisters in the North in the solid marks of respect they are about to show this distinguished veteran, who has grown gray in their service and is about retiring from an arduous profession with honor and an unimpeachable character but a most slender fortune.[30]

Tickets to the Parquette and Dress Circle were advertised at three dollars, but were cheaper for the boxes and gallery.

A neat address, composed by George E. Chase and delivered by Mrs. George Barrett, contributed to the gala atmosphere of the May evening on which Priscilla was introduced to Cooper's Southern friends. Like the abler couplets of Woodworth, written for the New York benefit, these review Cooper's triumphs. They conclude with an apt reference to Priscilla.

> . . . and to you
> Tonight he gives his own loved daughter too.
> Receive her kindly from the old man's hand
> And cherish into life this blossom of our land.[31]

Priscilla must have liked the elegant appearance of the New Orleans audience, for the ladies wore evening dress and the atmosphere was one of gentility and repose, often lacking in the nineteenth century American theatre. There are no letters and no journal dealing with this occasion, but with such a cast and such a welcome, it could not have been other than a happy experience for the young actress. Next day the papers were complimentary. The *Advertiser* reprinted in full the favorable reviews of the New York *Evening Post,* and added this statement:

> We have delayed thus long in alluding to the Cooper Festival awaiting the final settlement of the concerns of the committee, which we publish this day. The amount produced is comparatively small; this may be partly attributed to the low price of the seats and the money pressure which influences everything, more or less.
>
> The Soiree was a brilliant one, such as is rarely or never witnessed. The assemblage of beauty and fashion was greater than we ever saw on any similar occasion. The various performances went off with much eclat, and everybody appeared well satisfied.
>
> A similar benefit, we believe, is to be given the veteran in Mobile.[32]

The published reports of the various committees suggest that financially the occasion was a disappointment, but $1,636.37 for one night's acting seemed riches to Priscilla;[33] and Cooper, flattered by public favor and pleased by much kindness and hospitality, wrote the chairman of the committee who had the festival in charge a gracious letter.[34]

On April 21 Cooper had another benefit in which appeared his "interesting daughter, Miss P. E. Cooper." Forrest starred in the after piece, *The Orphan of Geneva,* but played in *Virginius* a minor role, generously yielding to the older actor and his daughter their hour of triumph.[35] It may be presumed that the house was crowded and that the girls and their father left, feeling grateful that the tour was proving more successful than they had dared to hope.

They probably played in Pittsburgh on their way home. Wemyss lists them as among the attractions of the frontier theatre during 1834, its third season, but assigns no date for their appearance.[36] In her letter to Jim written in February before they started their travels, Priscilla had promised that they would return in time for his graduation. It would not be in character for Cooper to disappoint himself or the girls in fulfilling the intention. They undoubtedly reached home in good time to spend June Week at The Point. No matter how happy the reunion, they were inevitably saddened by the absence of their mother, who had looked forward to the occasion as the fulfillment of long cherished hopes.

According to Ireland's *Memoir,* Priscilla and her father played in Baltimore at some time during 1834 and in Philadelphia in September of that year.[37] A few loose sheets torn from one of Mary Grace's journals deal with a week's engagement in Washington, December 12 through December 20.[38]

The complicated journey from Bristol to the Capital, as she described it, involved taking "a steamboat, then the railroad, and then a steamboat to Baltimore." There they caught the stage to Washington. Since they had gone to bed hungry, they had appetites for buckwheat cakes next morning—good ones, the girls found, for their hotel, Gadsby's, was the best in Washington. They express no dissatisfaction with their accommodations, though Fanny Kemble scorned the place in her journal as a scramble of wooden galleries, rambling passages, and innumerable staircases and doors.[39] It must have been drafty and not too luxurious in the sleety and disagreeable weather which Mary Grace notes in her journal.

The girls went sightseeing the next day—climbed to the top of the Capitol, went to the House of Representatives, sat in Calhoun's and Preston's chairs in the Senate chamber and longed to steal a pen as a souvenir. They were much impressed by the White House. Mary Grace remarked:

> How beautiful it is. I like the appearance of it and the Capitol being on opposite hills; they seem to overlook and protect the city. Think the President has no right to such a palace.

Possibly Mary Grace's criticism of Jackson, who she thought lived in too great splendor, would have been less severe if she had known that her sister, who was to play that night in the shabby little theatre with a company like something out of Hogarth, would in a few short years be completely at home in the White House, and as the official hostess of the president entertain foreign ministers and ambassadors as gracefully and simply as she played upon the stage.

Priscilla now had letter perfect the parts of Juliana in *The Honeymoon,* Juliet in *Romeo and Juliet,* Beatrice in *Much Ado about Nothing,* Mrs. Beverly in *The Gamester,* as well as that of Virginia. She went to rehearsal each morning with her father. Mary Grace always accompanied her to the theatre in the evening and brought her home. Before they went to bed each night they wrote in their journals. Mary Grace rarely mentioned her father's acting, but of Priscilla's performance there was always something flattering to record.

"Priss played Beatrice. Looked beautifully and played delightfully."

"Played Mrs. Beverly. Looked most graceful and elegant. With feeling."

Though the weather was bad and people did not come to the theatre in large numbers, this last engagement of 1834 rounded out a profitable year for the new venture. When their week was up, they went home, apparently almost cheerful, to spend Christmas with the children.[40]

4

THE CURTAIN FALLS

1835-1838

PRISCILLA and her father did not blaze a wide trail in the periodicals of the day after 1835, for by that time their appearing together had ceased to be a novelty. Their presence in the theatre was apparently not considered newsworthy in the large cities in the East. However, so long as they were playing in New York or Philadelphia, it is possible to follow their Odyssean wanderings by checking the rather generalized statements of Ireland's *The Professional Life of Thomas Abthorpe Cooper* against the more specific information to be found in Odell's *Annals of the New York Stage* or Wilson's *A History of the Philadelphia Theatre.* Unfortunately their engagements were oftenest in the provinces, where there was little dramatic reporting; so it is necessary in telling the story of the next few years to rely very largely on the correspondence and the journals of the Coopers themselves.

We know from a letter written by Mrs. Caroline Eliza Raoul, a friend in South Carolina, that they were in New Orleans and Charleston in the early spring of 1835.[1] Both Ireland and Wilson record a week's engagement in Philadelphia at the Walnut Theatre in May.[2] There in compliment to Priscilla, Sheridan Knowles, the English actor who wrote *Virginius,* played opposite her as Icilius. He must have made an unlikely looking Roman, being, so the diarist Philip Hone says, "a red-faced little fellow, with an appearance of joviality . . . a smack of Irish brogue . . . and the manners of a sea captain."[3]

Fortunately, by this time Priscilla, a seasoned trouper, had learned to take her fellow-actors as she found them. Later in the year she acted Lady Randolph to Mrs. Hamblin's Young Norval without flicking an eyelash, though even Mary Grace laughed at the pathetic scenes between the mother, aged nineteen, and the son, played by a matron of undetermined years. Priscilla's devoted sister apologizes for her levity, saying that as long as "Priss" was alone she imagined her as Lady Randolph completely; but when she contrasted her with the son, it was rather a stretch of the imagination.[4]

This episode is to be found in a tattered copy book, Mary Grace's journal, the only surviving one of many such volumes kept by the Cooper girls on tour, and the most satisfactory of all records of Priscilla's life on the stage. In it we have gossipy accounts of engagements in New York, Albany, Philadelphia, Baltimore, and Washington, from July 4 to December 18, 1835. Unfortunately, during the days in Washington Mary Grace had a toothache, and in Philadelphia she was greatly upset by the disturbing presence of a former lover, who fascinated and repelled her by his indifference. Priscilla and her father are occasionally crowded off the pages of the journal by the author's preoccupation with her own problems; but most of the time she is admirably satisfactory as a diarist, omitting nothing a biographer would wish to know.

The first entry is headed Bristol, the Fourth of July, 1835, which gala day the younger Coopers celebrated patriotically by setting off a great bunch of firecrackers.[5] Priscilla and Mary Grace were apparently comfortably adjusted to the tempo of home life, when Cooper suddenly announced his and Priscilla's departure for the West. Mary Grace was to stay at home, presumably for the sake of economy or possibly to take care of the children, who were to have a holiday from Miss Chapman's school in Holmesburg, which they reluctantly and irregularly attended. When a few days before her departure Priscilla went in the carriage to bring them home, she delighted them and their schoolmates by acting for them.[6]

She and Mary Grace tried to carry on the education of their charges in the tradition Mary Fairlie Cooper had established for her daughters—one in which neither the social graces nor the solid domestic virtues were neglected. Between tours, life in the two houses was much the same as it had been in their mother's lifetime. Mary Grace often rose at dawn to practice on the piano or study French. She was busy all day with the instruction of the younger girls, with needlework, or with supervision of the household. Priscilla, less diligent about domestic concerns, inspired her little sisters to emulation of her talents. They edited under her supervision *Paul Pry,* the family newspaper, which she and Mary Grace agreed had seen its best days and was becoming abominably stupid. Priscilla read aloud to them and urged them to produce their own plays. She helped them to write verses, and was interested in all their amusements. Olivia and Julia were more amenable to influence and instruction than Virginia and Louisa, the two youngest; but occasionally they were all very naughty.[7] On such occasions, the elder sisters invoked their mother's gentle spirit, prayed for heavenly guidance, and reasoned with the culprits, without resorting to any severer discipline.

The sort of life the Coopers led was not easy on anybody—snatches of time in Bristol during which the Cooper children had the attention and affection they needed; and then long absences during which they were neglected. Mary Grace and Priscilla found their responsibilities a heavy burden on their young shoulders. When they were together they managed fairly well, but when Priscilla went away alone both girls felt lost. It had been two years since their mother's death; and although neither of them was given to the melancholy considered becoming to maidens of the period, they needed the comfort of each other's presence. Priscilla, always reluctant to leave her elder sister, seems to have been especially distressed when she and her father set out at noon on the morning of July 24, 1835. That night Mary Grace, usually so cheerful and self-reliant, wrote in her journal that she felt "truly desolate."

She was troubled about Priscilla, who always needed her "in the minor department," for help in dressing her hair and keeping her costumes in order. She was disturbed about the probability of her taking cold. "Priss will sit by the window when the wind is blowing northeasterly. . . ."[8] After weeks of loneliness and anxiety, she was greatly relieved to get a letter from the travelers early in August, "enthusiastic as regards Niagara," but critical of everything else on the Northern tour.[9]

It was with no desire to rival her sister but rather to fill the emptiness caused by her absence that Mary Grace undertook humbly and seriously to improve herself. She practiced diligently on piano and guitar, till she could play "The Messenger Bird" with sentiment and "The Chieftain" with spirit. She tried her accomplishments out at several parties and on a number of the people who dropped in, for there were many visitors.

Among the most eligible of the gentlemen callers was Gratz Moses, a young man of wealth and position. He was the nephew of the beautiful Rebecca Gratz, whom Sully painted any number of times and whom Scott used as the model for Rebecca in *Ivanhoe.* She had often visited the Hoffmans in New York, and had shared with Mary Fairlie, Ann and Matilda Hoffman, Irving's admiration for the group which he called his "special girls." Mary Grace was glad to see Mr. Gratz; but she did not think him handsome, for he wore whiskers. "Those abominations!"[10]

The most welcome of the guests was her brother, Jim, who came between assignments to duty at remote army posts, "looking sunburned but sweet as ever." He was obviously disappointed at Priscilla's absence from home. Mary Grace, feeling herself a poor substitute for her livelier sister, tried hard to be gay and amusing; but Jim spent most of his time somewhere else and left sooner than he had intended.

Shortly after his departure on August 21, Cooper arrived without Priscilla, who had stayed over for a day in New York. She sent her journal on by her father so that Mary Grace would know by the time she reached home how little she had enjoyed this trip without her.[11]

When the weary traveler came the next day, Mary Grace was alarmed at how pale she looked, and lamented the fact that there was no chance for rest and relaxation; they must begin immediately energetic preparation for an important ten-day engagement in New York at the Bowery Theatre. The packing done, the children provided for, they got off to New York a day before their opening, September 4, so they could settle themselves at Mrs. McGaw's boarding house and make ready for the strenuous time ahead.

Mrs. McGaw welcomed them effusively. She seemed anxious to impress the girls with the fact that they were far from the first celebrities she had known. They were interested in her chatter about people she had worked for in England, among them Mrs. Radcliffe, in whose home she had been during the composition of *The Mysteries of Udolpho.* "She used to lie for hours by the side of a little stream and meditate," said Mrs. McGaw. And as for "Monk" Lewis, another of her acquaintances, he was "the most primitive man she ever saw."[12]

Priscilla listened somewhat absently to the loquacious woman. Her mind was filled with prognostications that this, her second appearance before the most critical audience in America, would be a failure. As the curtain rose on the opening night, she felt sure that her performance as Miss Dorillon in *Wives as They Were* would disgrace them all. A contagion of panic affected Mary Grace, who sat in a private box with Julia and John Fairlie, her aunt and uncle, uneasily aware of the faintness of the applause.[13] But it was not until the papers came out the next morning that they realized fully how well-founded Priscilla's forebodings had been. The critics complained that Cooper was dull and languid. The *Knickerbocker Magazine* politely suggested that he was too old for the roles he attempted; and Priscilla, though sweet and pretty, too young and inexperienced.

In many things the former Cooper recalled to our minds his ancient power; but we could not help thinking ever and anon,

"Alas!—*he is old, now!*" Miss Cooper needs only experience and a greater development of her physical and mental powers, to become all that her friends hope for her. As yet, she is but "a bud of promise."[14]

When *Damon and Pythias* went no better the next evening, Mary Grace, refusing to place the blame on Priscilla, wrote in her journal:

It is a great misfortune that the company is so bad they cannot get up the plays that she plays best. Priss played Hermione very well.[15]

Cooper seemed unaware of disapproval. In expansive mood he took his pretty daughters shopping. When they went into a store to buy cheap gloves, he liked the clerk who waited on them so well that he bought them each a shawl. Then he took them to Stewart's, the smartest shop in town, and helped them select the material for several dresses.

The New York audience had not seen Priscilla as Mrs. Beverly, Juliana, Hermione and Desdemona; and as the week progressed, they seemed pleased with the enlarged scope of her repertoire and applauded so enthusiastically that the sisters grew less tense. They both determined that when Priscilla played for the first time the following week as Lady Teazle in *School for Scandal,* no carelessness on their part should mar the performance. Priscilla studied Lady Teazle's lines in every spare moment and Mary Grace heard her recite the speeches over and over again while she worked on the costumes. After the play they felt great satisfaction that Priscilla acted well and looked pretty in a new hat.[16] All in all, the engagement that had started off so unpromisingly bade fair to end surprisingly well.

So far as was possible in a boarding house, the Coopers amused each other and kept to themselves, for they found the curiosity of their fellow guests a bore, especially that of a Miss Dempster, who was full of impertinent questions about Priscilla's life on the stage: "Do you have fun?" she asked. "Do you ever wear men's clothes?" "Have you ever worn the kilt?" One night she kept the girls up long after their bedtime with her foolish talk.

She asked the young actress to play a ghost for her, and Priscilla jumped into bed and said she would show her how "to give up the ghost."[17]

Games of blind man's buff and "discovering each other phrenologically" went on in Mrs. McGaw's parlor every night after supper. "Putting phrenology to an admirable use," Mary Grace commented caustically. However, she and Priscilla bought and read Combe's book, which was the last word on how to tell character by the shape of the head. They wanted to be well-informed about this mysterious "science" which was the latest fad.[18] Fortunately Priscilla's professional duties were a perfect excuse for absenting themselves from amusements they thought vulgar. When their presence was not required at the Bowery, she and Mary Grace took a busman's holiday by going to other theatres to see experienced actresses like Mrs. Abbot or Miss Wheatley. Mary Grace always loyally declared them greatly inferior to Priscilla in the same roles.[19]

Rehearsals in the morning and performances at night kept the sisters so busy that they saw very little of the Fairlies, except Julia, who came almost every evening to the theatre and often in the morning to Mrs. McGaw's to see her nieces. Maria Fairlie tried to improve upon her bad behavior at the time of her granddaughter's debut the year before by making them welcome in the new home on Christopher Street, a less pretentious establishment than the Cortlandt Street residence but one in which a semblance of the former elegance was maintained. Mary Grace writes of having there for dinner such luxuries as celery, oysters, and champagne. Priscilla, weary from her exertions, or perhaps resentful that her father was not included in the Fairlies' hospitable attentions, seldom accepted any of the many invitations extended them and had to be persuaded to pay dutiful visits to see her grandmother.

Both girls appreciated the fact that the friends in New York were especially cordial. Mrs. Nicholas, Mrs. Morris, Gratz Moses, and Miss Moses called several times during the week—and many others whom Mary Grace indicated in her journal by baffling

MISS COOPER AS HELENA.

COOPER as PIERE
"Whence these vile Chains?"
Venice Preserv'd.

COOPER IN CAPTAIN

initials. The visit of Mr. Verplanck and Charles Hoffman she reports in full, possibly because the young men came from families with whom the Fairlies had been intimate for two generations. One friendship dated back to the period at the close of the Revolution when Guilian C. Verplanck and Major Fairlie had interested themselves in founding the Society of the Cincinnati; and the other, to the days of Mary Fairlie's girlhood when she and Ann Hoffman, Charles's sister, were inseparable. Hoffman enjoyed at the moment considerable reputation as a poet and as an editor of the *Knickerbocker Magazine*. Possibly he had no hand in the comment of that periodical which praised Priscilla in lukewarm terms as "a bud of promise," for on the occasion of their visit both gentlemen were full of extravagant compliments. Mary Grace wrote them down, since Priscilla was not there to receive them in person: "The most graceful, the most ladylike, the most agreeable, charming creature in the world."[20] A few days later Charles Hoffman met Maria Fairlie on the street and pleased the old lady by saying her granddaughter was "the most fascinating creature" he ever beheld.[21]

The Coopers listened greedily to the flattery of their friends and tried to ignore the silent disapproval of the press. They were feeling cheerful by the time of the final performance of the engagement, *Romeo and Juliet.* Their trunks were packed except for the costumes for Priscilla's benefit that evening. Not until they read the announcement in the paper at breakfast did they know that the play had been changed to *The Honeymoon.* They had to unpack, get costumes cleaned and pressed—do any number of chores. By the time the curtain went up they were in such a state they did not seem to notice, as several spectators did, that Cooper took no part in the dance, in which as Duke Aranza he had once won praise for his grace and agility.[22] No one was aware, apparently, that only once more—and then for one night in Hamblin's benefit (November 24, 1835)—was Cooper to tread the stage in the city where in 1797, thirty-eight years before, he had made his first bow to a New York audience. The actors with whom he had played in those early years—Mrs.

Merry, Fennell, Warren, Mrs. Oldmixon—had been dead for many years. He had, as Odell says, "stayed too long before a public notoriously fickle."[23]

Happily unaware of the finality of their departure, on Monday, September 28, 1835, the family started for Albany. One of Cooper's faithful admirers, Col. Walton, saw them off. He begged Priscilla not to treat him as Fanny Kemble had. She had pretended to be interested in his conversation and later had put him in her book as a bore and "a button-holder." The girls tried to be very kind indeed to the old man, feeling that it was not difficult to outdo the Kembles in courtesy. They had read Fanny's journal and had been shocked by the unkind things she had written about people who had entertained her and her father.

The river boat was packed with all kinds of people. Mary Grace and Priscilla, after a restless night in the women's cabin, were glad to reach their destination and to go to the hospitable inn in Albany, where they had tea before a bright fire in the comfortable parlor. There they met and enjoyed chatting with old Judge Miller, who had known Major Fairlie long, long ago, and thought him the handsomest man he had ever seen.[24]

In ordinary times Albany was a good theatre town, but now money was tight. In spite of the poor houses they played to, the Coopers managed to enjoy themselves. They took a long ride to see the falls of the Mohawk, noting with pleasure the beauty of the autumn woods. The Yateses, Maria Fairlie's brother's family, came to call and were most affectionate and cordial. Mrs. Yates invited them to dinner—"Very nice. Champagne, wine, etc."—and she and Mr. Yates took them to see the "shaking Quakers," a cult founded by Mother Ann. Mary Grace sums up their creed briefly: "Christ came into the world to save *Man*kind; Mother Ann, to save *woman*kind."[25]

Though Priscilla played a heavy program—Desdemona, Miss Dorillon, Juliet, and Hermione—she was not too weary or too busy to see old friends in the town. According to Mary Grace, she chattered away like a magpie when they passed the evening with the Bloodworths. "Conversation was the order of the evening. Priss and Mrs. B. had us all for listeners." Almost reluctantly they left on Friday afternoon. The boat was not crowded, and the scenery along the Hudson so lovely that the girls hated to go to bed and miss part of the trip.[26]

On arriving in New York they went directly from the Albany boat to that for Bristol. They were half starved by the time Cooper brought their makeshift breakfast, and they attacked "hard-boiled eggs, crackers and molasses cake" with good appetites.

When they reached home they found Olivia and Julia, the elder of the young Coopers, waiting on the wharf. Everyone was excited and happy at the reunion around the dinner table that evening. It was comforting to be together, even if the three travelers could stay only two days before they were off again to play at the Walnut Street Theatre in Philadelphia.

There they lodged with Mrs. Reynolds, and Mary Grace went to work immediately lining trains and putting in sleeves in order to have everything in order for October 15, their opening night.[27] She was too unhappy during the following days to note the cheerful aspects of the visit. The lover whom she does not name kept her upset. He came every day to call, but she was wretchedly self-conscious when she was in the room with him and took great pains to be reserved and even unfriendly. Priscilla went her sunny way, being casually pleasant to the young man and turning an indifferent ear to his compliments. So complete was the understanding between the sisters that in Mary Grace's misery there is no hint of jealousy.

Toward the end of the engagement at the Walnut Theatre she had her emotions under control, and there is a spirited account of how on October 24, the children and the servants came up from Bristol to Cooper's benefit, *Rule a Wife and Have a Wife.* Although it was a version from which everything that could be shocking had been eliminated, Cooper's acting as Leon and Priscilla's as Estifania made Louisa, the baby, cry and left Susan Poor, the maid, "completely bewildered."

Mary Grace wrote the following account of the evening:

Went to the theatre . . . Very good house. Priss admirable. Everybody complimented her. After the play they called Pa for a long time. Hissed the music so that we could not hear a note, and when the curtain rose for the farce, they hissed the actor off the stage and Pa had to come forth. He apologized for having kept them waiting. Said if he had expected the honor he would not have commenced undressing himself. As it was he was obliged to wait until he had completely changed his dress. Thanked them for the kindness of many, many years. Said he must soon go to "that country from whose bourn no traveler returns" (looking as well as he ever did). But if he should a few more times again appear before them, he hoped to be received as he had now. . . .

That night Papa gave up his room to the children and lay down on the sofa. The rest slept at our feet. . . .[28]

There is no need to describe in detail the one or two night stands they played in Washington, Baltimore, and Washington again, November 2 to November 12. A succession of disappointing experiences was climaxed by a quarrel resulting in a lawsuit between Cooper and the manager of the theatre in the Capital City. Not at all pleased with the way they had been treated, they made a hasty departure for home.

After having been on the road for two months, they found Bristol a peaceful haven. The girls went for long walks in the crisp November weather to hunt for "percimines."[29] They all played games around the fire at night or visited the neighbors. Priscilla must have felt her heart sink when on the nineteenth of November Cooper told her to get ready to go South within a month. By this time one lodging house, one theatre, one rehearsal, one performance must have come to seem like another; and the traveling-about, which had once been exciting, was weary routine.

This December tour was an especial hardship, for Christmas was coming. She hated leaving Mary Grace, for she knew her elder sister liked especially to go to Charleston to see the Raouls and to New Orleans to see the Barries. Mary Grace cried as she packed the costume trunks in "the other house." She attributed her tears to the bitter weather. No one felt much holiday spirit when Priscilla and Cooper, both with colds, started out in a blizzard on their long journey.[30] They went by canal boat to Chesapeake City, and then by steamboat for an overnight ride to Baltimore. There Cooper usually stayed at Barnum's, a rendezvous for theatrical people, and boarded the boat the next morning for Norfolk. From that point on they went by coach and private vehicle across country through Virginia and into the Carolinas. The trip involved eight days of discomfort and exposure; the food was poor and the accommodations at the inns along the way, almost primitive.[31]

While they were away a letter arrived for Cooper which Mary Grace could hardly wait to see opened. It was from Mary Shelley, and though such letters were not rarities, they were always the occasion of considerable excitement; for the girls made a cult of Shelley worship. All too frequently communications from the Godwins were requests for money; nevertheless they seemed to Mary Grace and Priscilla glorified by having come from someone who knew the poet.[32] Priscilla's admiration for his works was lifelong. When she was an old woman, one of her grandsons ran away from home, taking with him only his toothbrush and a volume of Shelley's poetry. She assured his frantic parents that no harm could come to a boy with such cleanly habits and such good taste in literature.[33]

On the travellers' return the letter proved interesting. Mary Shelley wrote to Cooper asking him to arrange with American booksellers for the sale of a book she was at work on—probably *Faulkner,* published in 1837. She was outspoken in her dislike of Sir Timothy Shelley, her father-in-law, and discussed her personal affairs freely as with an intimate friend.

We are wholly dependent on my husband's father during his life and he is narrow-minded and niggardly. Therefore my life has been by no means an easy one. When he dies Percy and I shall be well off, but he continues to live and may for years longer. While he lives I must remain here. When he dies the thousand cares attendant on our embarrassed property will still retain me.

Because of her interest in her son's future, she refused an invitation to come to America to visit the Coopers.

> Percy is now seventeen. He is all I could wish, but I would not separate from him for the world—and his education must be finished at one of our universities. He will not be unworthy either of his grandfather or father. His understanding is clear and his integrity and steadiness singularly great, joined as these qualities are to a high spirit and great cheerfulness of disposition. I do not expect him to make a figure, for he has no ambition, but feel certain that he will be a happy man.[34]

She went on to say that Godwin's widow, her stepmother, was in financial difficulties. It had always given Cooper satisfaction to make generous gifts to his foster father and his family, and it must have cost his pride a pang to ignore this hint—if indeed he did. It is hard to see, however, by what miracle he could have raised funds to give away, for he and Priscilla were earning no more than a bare livelihood by their joint efforts.

They were so poor there was no longer pretense on Cooper's part that they were eagerly sought after. In a man less proud it would seem strange that he never considered humbling himself sufficiently to seek work as a stock actor, but preferred the arduous life he and his daughter led to giving up stardom. As the times grew harder, and theatre after theatre closed, his efforts to earn a living became more strenuous. He must have written many letters like the following one, addressed to F. C. Wemyss, manager of the Pittsburgh Theatre, October, 1835:

> My dear Sir:
>
> The last time I was at Pittsburgh was election time. Could I be of any service now these troubles are over? My list alone, you know. With my daughter it is extended several parts—*School for Scandal, Damon and Pythias, Rule a Wife, Romeo and Juliet, Othello, Hunchback, Wives and Maids.* A line in two or three days will oblige.
>
> Yours respectfully,
> Thomas A. Cooper[35]
>
> Bristol, near Philadelphia

That so many of the requests addressed to relatively unimportant managers in unimportant places met with response should be considered no mean success when viewed against the dark background of the depression of 1836, which ushered in the panic of 1837. The Coopers kept busy during a period when idleness and unemployment were the order of the day. From Ireland's biography of Cooper we know of two weeks in New Orleans, where he won critical acclaim for his acting in *Macbeth;* of appearances in Savannah, Richmond, Boston, and Philadelphia. The six performances at the Walnut Street Theatre in September of 1836 marked the end of an epoch. Father and daughter were to act no more in the large cities in the East, but henceforth only in the South and the West, where they could still command an audience.[36]

Letters from Priscilla during this period are cheerful, hardly from ignorance of the situation, possibly from a desire not to trouble Mary Grace and the girls needlessly. From Augusta, Georgia, on February 28, 1836, she sent an account of her adventures, from which she omitted any mention of hardships:

> The last week I spent in Savannah was charming. I went to five parties and was a little of a d—d particular belle. My benefit was crowded, and three companies of soldiers, dressed in their uniforms, attended the theatre, entirely out of compliment to me. The pit was filled by them and ten boxes. All the nicest young men in town belonging to them. After the play, which was *The Hunchback*—and which I played in Savannah four times, being considered magnificent in it—after the play I was serenaded all night nearly by the . . . bands of the companies. In fact, they say I am the only person that has roused the young men of Savannah for many a long day. And I have made them chivalrous, romantic, and everything else. One gentleman there undertook to repeat all the compliments he heard made of me. I will tell you a few—no, I won't either! I'd sound too conceited. I'll just tell you one that made me leave my heart with its perpetrator. Mr. Somebody said to Mr. Ward, "Oh, do look at Mrs. Jackson. How pretty she looks!"
>
> "Don't ask me to look at anyone. I am looking at the spot where Miss Cooper *was!*"

Is not that poetical? And if you could see and know Mr. Ward, you would fall in love with him. He is handsome and talented to a wonderful degree and has read quantities of novels.[37]

Throughout the remainder of 1836 Priscilla's letters home maintain a tone of forced gaiety, which was intended to be reassuring to those who loved her. A brief bulletin written from Norfolk in October is typical.

I played every night I was in Richmond except two, one of them Sunday and the other I had a chill.

My benefit was Julia. Such a beautiful house—everybody in the place—really crowded, still only four hundred dollars! . . . As to my being a favorite, there is no doubt of it. I am tired of telling you about flowers. Every day a bouquet, and generally two or three—five serenades, really, during the ten days, such kindness, attention and devotion from everyone. My admirers passing my window a dozen times a day just to get one glance. But I won't say any more about it, for you are all laughing at me now.

In spite of her efforts to seem happy there are passages which indicate that she was lonely and homesick:

How is Miss Hannah? [The cook] I wish I had a loaf of her bread. And Hero? [The dog] I wish I could see a wag of his tail.[38]

Before the election of Van Buren in November of 1836 everyone hoped the new President would find a way to avert the economic disaster toward which the country moved; but by 1837 there was no confidence in the government, and Van Buren was represented in cartoons as a fop who drank champagne at a table laden with luxuries, while the people starved.

The Coopers did not starve but they felt the pinch of poverty. Priscilla, at home in Bristol between infrequent engagements, wrote to Mary Grace, visiting Mrs. Raoul in South Carolina, the grim truth about their situation:

May 17, 1837

. . . We have radishes and salad—not roses and strawberries. The latter I shall not hope to taste this year, for economy is the order of the day. One pound of butter lasts us two days. We eat rye bread, burn one candle. Pa gets shaved once in two days and by the month. [We] wash ourselves only once a week as the Delaware is red, eat nothing but bacon and potatoes for dinner, with an occasional lone dumpling to give weight to the repast. . . .

Our business in Baltimore was so utterly wretched that Papa could not afford to go for you. We arrived there Sunday morning at six, so you may imagine that without anyone to assist me in anything I was rather hurried. I got over it in my usual way—a kind of desperation. Our houses were most miserable. Excepting at our benefits we did not make one sou and then only just cleared our expenses. Hard times, banks breaking, merchants failing and strong fear of negro and Irish mobs. This latter keeping all the fathers of families in their houses after nightfall.

I sit from six till eight, before the candles are lighted, at the window, thinking of nothing but when we again shall meet. I have made up my mind, however petulant and ill-natured I may seem to you, that I love you better than any one else in the world. I always thought I loved Jim the most; but you have both been away from me at the same time, and I feel that the sight of you would be more welcome to me.

By way of making the outlook yet more gloomy, Cooper was ill and was not a patient invalid.

Pa today has one of his attacks—came on all of a sudden. He can't talk at all, of course, and is moaning and groaning, sputtering and sniffling and half coughing at the same time. As cross—Oh, genius! He writes down everything he wants in a scrawl impossible to read.[39]

Priscilla could find no cheerful news for Mary Grace; she could, however, assure her that their predicament was by no means uncommon. She recounts for her in this same letter the complaints of Mrs. Caton, who had entertained her when she was last in Baltimore. This distinguished lady, whose three daughters had married into the peerage—a duke, a marquis, and a count respectively—should have been safe, if anyone was, from the effects of an unsettled economy.

I had the pleasure of making the acquaintance of Mrs. Caton. She was very kind to me and talked so delightfully I was perfectly charmed with her. She told me all about everyone I wanted to see. I really imagined as she talked of all the great people that she was personally introducing me to them. You may slightly imagine the general poverty of the city when I tell you this:

Mrs. Caton, you know, is one of the richest persons in the Union. From stocks falling, property decreasing in value, merchants' failing, banks breaking, she says she actually has not money to have her house cleaned.[40]

From meager source material we find that in the face of difficulties worse than Mrs. Caton's the Coopers struggled on, not without some small degree of satisfaction to themselves and their audiences.

Dr. Irving in "Reminiscences of the Charleston Stage" describes one occasion when the Coopers acted before an audience that overflowed the theatre. Unfortunately, they were not the chief attraction.

On the 19th December [1837] Ellien [sic] Free made her first appearance in Charleston in the play of *The Hunchback* and continued her engagement until the 4th of January when Mr. and Miss Cooper opened in *Much Ado about Nothing*. During this engagement the Indian chiefs from Florida, Osceola and others, visited the theatre, on which occasion so great was the curiosity of the community to see how these uncivilized men would regard 'the mimic scene' that no less a sum than $1,200 was received at the doors—a nice little crumb for the manager.[41]

Priscilla told her children in later years that she was glad to escape from the theatre that night without being scalped, for the Redskins sat without smiling, apparently displeased by the play.

Of a more flattering response in Richmond, she wrote a lengthy account, March 18, 1837, to Mary Grace.

Every newspaper here has some trifling praise of me, such as calling me chaste, dutiful, elegant, ladylike, etc., but none worth sending. I will give you an idea of what they are generally by one in particular.

"We doubt whether it has been the good fortune of many ever to have witnessed a more affecting piece of acting than that of Miss Cooper on Wednesday evening as Miss Dorillon.

There was in the delineation of this character a freshness of conception, a delicacy and a truth to nature which made way directly to the heart and brought the unbidden tear to many an eye. This effect was observed both upon young and old. . . . We hope that the lady who fulfills as well in real as in scenic life the part of a daughter so exemplary, etc., etc."

This is rather damning with faint praise. Moreover, I don't know any of the editors, so I don't know why they mention me at all.

. . . Richmond is a beautiful place, the prettiest city I think I have ever seen in the South. Various residences are absolute palaces. . . . I am quite attended here, tho I have been to no parties; I have forsworn them. They are so expensive. I had five japonicas sent me in two days, all by different persons. What do you think of that? A japonica is considered the most beautiful present you can send a lady. Violets without number adorn my table, to say nothing of *billet doux.* I have received one admirable offer that I should like to accept, tho I don't much care for the person. . . .

I am learning to sew on purpose to make me a frock . . . and you know that is my strong point. We have not yet got our box, and I assure you I look rather shabbily, particularly as the weather is quite springlike and my coat has become rather sweltering. However, I always pretend I have a severe cold, and am obliged to put on as much as possible.[42]

Her gallant pretense that she did not mind giving up parties and wearing her old coat in warm weather to hide her shabby dress must have distressed her absent sister, who always looked after Priscilla's clothes. Mary Grace stayed at the Raouls' in South Carolina for the better part of a year not entirely from choice but because her father could not make the financial arrangements for her trip home. His embarrassment was not due entirely to lack of funds but in some measure to the very serious economic upheaval which had upset the value of the currency. The country was flooded with "shinplasters," due bills issued by merchants, butchers, and tradesfolk, as well as by borough and city governments. These were promises to pay on demand, very few of which were redeemable.[43] Priscilla tried to explain to Mary Grace in a letter, apparently written in the spring of 1837:

You have heard, I suppose, of the small bills the corporation of Philadelphia has been issuing, like the old continental money —bills for two pence, six pence. And specie has entirely stopped. Papa has immortalized himself in Bristol by preventing all the people from taking or giving these notes, showing them all the danger and explaining all the affair to them—which, my love, he will to you when you come home, as he does to me five hundred times a day.

Pa says there is a steamboat expected to sail from Philadelphia to Charleston everyday, and he will go to a broker's and get Charleston money to send you to bring you home, for a Northern bank note will not pass in the South. Pa will write in a day or two and give you his directions.[44]

The family in New York seemed to have realized only remotely the difficulties which the Coopers were experiencing that spring. Julia Fairlie, writing to her nephew, Jim Cooper, in March of 1837, took a very sanguine attitude towards Priscilla's career:

Speaking of Priss reminds me of a very complimentary notice of her which I saw in one of the papers. It was taken from one of the Savannah newspapers, speaking very highly of her dramatic talent, and (what was more gratifying to me) in highest terms of her private character, that she was entertained and noticed by "the most aristocratic society in Savannah, and that the ladies, to do her honor, went to her benefit in full dress, with flowers in their hair."

Poor, dear girl, it gives me much pleasure to hear of her meeting with such encouragement in her arduous duties, for if ever a girl was activated by high, noble and disinterested feelings, it is she.

In this same letter Julia Fairlie, whom the family had long ago given up to be an old maid like her sister Louisa, told Jim of her marriage to a Mr. Samuel G. Ogden, considerably her senior. She was apparently a quite indifferent bride.

. . . I had nothing whatever to do about the arrangements. Everything, even to ordering the cake, was done by Mr. Ogden. All that I had to do was to walk from Grove Street to St. John's Park —and, God knows, that was hard enough. I was on the point of turning back several times.[45]

In spite of her detached attitude, the match was a happy one, even from the viewpoint of Ogden's daughter, Anna Cora Ogden Mowatt, whose satirical attitude toward men and women in her famous play, *Fashion,* suggests that she would not be flattering in her estimate of a stepmother. In her autobiography she wrote most fondly of Julia Fairlie Ogden:

Such a striking contradiction was given to the old maxim that condemns stepmothers in the person of our second mother that her harmonious life ought almost to take away the reproach that attaches itself to that much-maligned class. The loadstar of her gentleness had attracted to itself the affections of all her husband's children. . . . She contributed four most sweet additions to our already extensive sisterhood.[46]

The letters of 1837 tell news from other members of the family besides Julia. Jim Cooper resigned that year from the army and started work as a construction engineer for the Western and Atlantic Railroad. The family were dismayed by this upheaval in his plans at a time when the prospects for advancement in any field were dim. And there was considerable excitement about Mary Grace, aged twenty-four, who finally returned from South Carolina engaged to Frederic Sebastian Raoul, the youngest son of Mrs. Caroline Eliza Raoul, whom she had been visiting. Not until two years later did they think of marriage, for as yet Frederic's position in the world was not established, and Mary Grace's duty to her father, Priscilla, and the children was not fully discharged.

The following year (1838) the Coopers had few regular engagements. They played in Charleston in the spring, and according to Hornblow were in Boston in September.[47] On October 29, 1838, Ireland says they played in Albany, together for the last time on any stage.[48] Stuck at the end of the fourth column on page two of the Albany *Argus* is a brief notice of their final appearance on that date:

Mr. Cooper and his talented and amiable daughter appear this evening in their celebrated characters of Benedict and Beatrice. The admirers of Shakespeare will, we are assured, find ample

remuneration for their attendance on the representation of this elegant comedy of the immortal bard.
C. W. Taylor, Manager
Curtain 7:00
Boxes 75c Pit 37½c Gal. 25c[49]

As the Coopers bowed in acknowledgement of the indifferent applause, and the curtain of the shabby theatre in Albany swept down like a funeral pall, Priscilla must have thought back to the brilliance of her debut in New York four and a half years before, and must have regretted this anticlimactic ending to her career. Her real sadness, however, would have been rather for her father than for herself. He was abdicating reluctantly, once and for all, claims to any consideration of greatness in a realm where he had once been supreme. She had never found acting a rewarding experience and had been more than half in love with the idea of retirement since she first set foot upon the stage. Moreover, she was only twenty-two and no tragedy is final to youth. But Cooper was old; and when a few months later he made an appearance in Charleston without his daughter, his friends thought him greatly changed; J. B. Irving says that he refused a benefit and apparently regarded that night's acting as his farewell to his profession.

He seemed to linger with peculiar interest among his early friends, putting off his departure from day to day, with feelings so unusually softened as to be remarked by everybody that knew him in his sterner days—it was a striking but sweetly pleasing contrast to that rather hard nature and to that dictatorial tone, attributed to him by many, at one period of his life. I had not been an indifferent observer of his chastened feelings. Contemplating him like Belisarius, standing up manfully, a noble ruin, amid the wreck and crash of his fallen fortunes, out of sincere sympathy for my old friend, and from a hint he gave me that it would be agreeable, I remained as much with him as other demands upon my time would permit, accompanying him at last to the ship to see him off.[50]

5

A LOVE IDYLL

1839-1844

Before Priscilla abandoned her career upon the stage, she had begun to long for the economic and emotional security a happy marriage brings. In a letter to Mary Grace, written in Richmond, March 18, 1837, she described wistfully the establishment of a friend.

> She lives near Richmond and is married to one of the innumerable Randolphs and resides at the most amazing house I ever saw. It is called Wilton and has been in the Randolph family for generation to generation. It is very old fashioned—such thick walls and such a wide, charming, romantic old hall hung round with antlers and powder flasks, shot bags, guns, pouches, etc. The parlors have old black oak panelling, and the walls are hung all round with the most dear, delightful, charming old family pictures, centuries old. Ladies in hoops and powder, gentlemen in wigs and satin coats. It is just the kind of place I should like to pass my life in and never step out of, particularly if I had Mr. Randolph in the bargain, for he is a very handsome young man, a true Virginia gentleman, fond of horses, dogs, his wife and baby. Which latter is a darling. . . .

Later in the same letter she remarks that if some one "with a large country establishment in Virginia, a good family name, and a handsome and good-natured person" should fall in love with her, she would not think his proposal "to be sneezed at."[1]

Apparently her challenge to fate was not to go unanswered;

for immediately, or shortly afterwards, she met Robert Tyler, the eldest son of John Tyler.[2] The youth, though not conventionally handsome, was tall and distinguished looking. He had graduated from the College of William and Mary in 1835, and was reading law in the office of Professor Beverley Tucker, in Williamsburg, where the Tylers were living at the time. He was regarded as an ambitious and promising young man. No family in the Tidewater was older or more respected than his. They had owned land there since the middle of the seventeenth century and had been prominent in public affairs in Virginia ever since. John Tyler and his father before him had been elected and re-elected state governor, an honor many Virginians regard as being second only to the Presidency of the United States. Certainly Robert Tyler was not a suitor "to be sneezed at." Moreover, the meeting between the two young people was dramatic enough to satisfy the heart of a girl who had played the part of heroines in stage romances.

The story they told their children—and there is no reason to doubt its truth—was that Robert went while he was on a visit in Richmond to see the famous actor, Cooper, play Othello. When Priscilla made her entrance as Desdemona, the audience rose to applaud, a sign of respect frequently paid the lovely young actress. After the rest sat down, Robert remained standing, wrapped in admiration. That same night he went backstage and asked her father's permission "to pay his addresses." He had at first sight fallen completely and helplessly in love.

It seems probable that this dramatic meeting took place on the evening of March 18, 1837, for Priscilla played Desdemona that night in Richmond. In a letter to Mary Grace written that morning she expressed a wish that her sister were there to help her curl the wig she was to wear for the part.[3] If this assumption be correct, then the courtship was no whirlwind affair; for the marriage did not take place until September of 1839. Judging by the tone of ten love letters, written in the spring and summer of 1839, two years later Robert was still ardent in pursuit of the lady. After the couple were publicly engaged and the Coopers

JOHN TYLER, PRESIDENT OF
THE UNITED STATES

BY GEORGE PETER ALEXANDER HEALEY

ROBERT TYLER

BY AN UNKNOWN ARTIST

were making what preparations they could for the wedding, he joked about the fact that Priscilla had refused him no less than six times.[4] As soon as they came to an understanding Priscilla wrote to him with reassuring regularity; she seemed to do nothing to upset him; but he was wildly jealous and excited. His passion was so intense that he resorted at times to verse. Even the prose of the letters is poetic:

> I solemnly swear that even if I would, I do not believe I could forget you. God knows I love you, and you only. I know no delight but in you. I have no breath itself but in you. The sun has no warmth or light if you are not with me. Night is truly darkness, gloomy darkness. . . .[5]
>
> When the moon shines brightly, and my favorite mocking bird in the garden sings to me, I always think of you. They are quiet and unassuming and innocent, yet full of loveliness like yourself, my Lissy. Don't you know I love you best because of an air of innocence about everything you say and do, which seems to be absolutely unconscious of wrong or evil. . . .[6]
>
> My God! how heavily the days drag on now. It appears to me there is an ordinary week comprehended between the rising and going down of the sun. When I get your miniature, however, I shall be better reconciled. I can't see why, although I know it will be so, for your image is indelibly traced upon my heart, and vividly before my mind, as if you were in real presence with me.[7]

Robert had the good fortune to be a remarkably articulate lover. He was, in fact, at work upon a volume of verse scheduled for immediate publication by Carey and Lea.[8] As soon as it was off the press, in September of 1839, Priscilla sent Julia Fairlie Ogden a copy, asking her to forward it for review to their friend, Hoffman, now an editorial writer for the *New-Yorker*. She had in reply interesting comment from Julia:

> Thank him in my name for the pleasure he has given me in reading his volume of beautiful poems. (The address is in your handwriting, and Mr. Tyler is probably unaware of its being sent) but *n'importe*. Thank him all the same.
>
> I admire the "Address to the Elements of the Beautiful" the most; I believe it is because they remind me of Wordsworth, par-

ticularly these very beautiful lines. When speaking of Nature's varied beauties, he says:

> "From boyhood's playful hour
> My passionate worship ye have always been,
> For in your fine existencies I have
> Ever felt that mystic spirit, which with
> The rare essence of the soul commingling,
> Lights up a dazzling flame immortal, never
> To be quench'd. . . ."

And in "The Last Man" I think the images of horror are extremely fine, exciting the same sensations of dread of those in "The Darkness" of Byron.[9]

This flattering criticism and the selection quoted from Robert Tyler's work suggest that his is derivative but graceful verse. He was later to win the admiration of the family circle and some critical praise by two additional works, *Ahasuerus* and *Medora's Dream*,[10] the favorable reception of which on the part of the public may have been influenced to some extent by the fact that by the time of their publication (1842) his father was the President of the United States.

He was by no means a great poet, but facility in the use of words is no handicap to a lover—particularly one separated from his beloved. Fortunately there have been preserved a few of the many letters he addressed to Priscilla Cooper. They were written in the spring and summer of 1839, just before he married her. Although they were the expression of a sensitive and high-minded young man, thoroughly imbued with the chivalric ideals of the Virginia gentleman of the nineteenth century, no modern girl could find fault with him as a lover. He addressed Priscilla always as an intellectual equal, asking her opinion about books and philosophical questions; he is grave and gay by turns; tender and mocking. He is never dissatisfied with anything she does or says but full of humble doubt that she can love him. If occasionally the style seems a little self-conscious or a trifle literary, it must be remembered that Robert Tyler was only twenty-three years old and that the extravagant promises he made Priscilla were fulfilled when he became her devoted husband.

The first of these eloquent love letters, dated March 15, 1839, was written after his return to Williamsburg from a happy visit with Priscilla in Bristol.

My passage down the river was not so fatiguing as I had anticipated. I met with several old and beloved friends, all men of sound honor, and the time, considering the woeful circumstance that my face was turned from you, passed almost pleasantly. I had an invitation to make one at a card-playing party (my favorite amusement, with one exception only of eating pickled oysters) but I felt not the slightest inclination to join. Can you tell me, my own dear, dear Lissy, what could have caused this indisposition, so unusual with me, to gambling convivially? There were only three ladies on board, two of whom thought it entirely proper (under the inducement doubtless of being with *me*) to stop at Jamestown. One of these fair damsels I very gallantly assisted to walk the plank. Now don't take me for a pirate. I only assisted her, with by no means an obsequious politeness, from the perils of water and storm to the dangers less in magnitude, it is true, of a rickety wharf.[11]

The tone of the letter is lover-like, but there seems to be as yet no formal engagement. It was later, while Priscilla was on a visit to Laura Towns in Petersburg that Robert persuaded her to marry him. He wrote on April 10 a letter to her at that address, filled with ecstatic memories of a recent meeting there. He took his responsibilities as a future husband so seriously that he proposed to give up the writing of verse as unprofitable and to devote himself hereafter to the law—a suggestion that Priscilla was supposed to repudiate—and probably did—although trifles indicate that she admired her lover's poetry only because it was his.

Robert's mother, Letitia Christian Tyler, had recently suffered a paralytic stroke, which had impaired her speech. She could not express her joy in words when she heard of the happy outcome of her son's courtship, but her actions were eloquent. Robert writes to Priscilla:

She met me and threw her arms around my neck and wept like a child. I need not, I know, even hint to you that you must love her dearly. She is more [glad] that I shall marry you than anyone else in the world. Love she sends as to a daughter.[12]

The Tylers seem to have welcomed the young actress into the family with no hint of aristocratic condescension, but eagerly, as if the penniless girl were bestowing an honor upon them. Priscilla had been so carefully protected and had behaved with such discretion while she was on the stage that no breath of censure had touched her. If it had, John Tyler, Sr. would have been outspoken in disapproval. (He forbade his own daughter's waltzing.) That he found no fault with Robert's choice of a wife speaks highly not only of Priscilla's innocent sweetness but of her reputation as well.

Robert took pains to let his "Lissy" know that he was proud to be her lover.

You don't know how much I am envied by my gentleman acquaintances. Maybe you had better kick me now and marry some better fellow among these aspiring gallants.[13]

On May 30, 1839, he transcribed at great length tributes from certain of his father's contemporaries:

I have heard of one or two compliments paid you lately, my Lissy, which have delighted me. You remember the gentleman, a member of the legislature, by the name of Barton, who was introduced to you in the theatre at Petersburg. I confess my feelings were not kindly to him, for I thought he treated the Governor badly last winter in the matter of the Senatorial election, but I am now disposed to like him much better. The old man [Robert's father] told me the other day of his having mentioned to him the fact of seeing us together, with the additional information that he thought I was pleased with you and moreover would in his opinion succeed in my addresses. He [Barton] then said that I would be as lucky as any mortal man could well be in such a choice, for that you, my own, *own* Lissy, were certainly the sweetest thing in the world; and that if he was a single man you would be his choice, providing you would marry him—An ounce of civit on such an ideal—before the whole world. John [Robert's brother, John Tyler, Jr.] told me yesterday that General —— declares that if he had a brother he had rather he should marry you than any other woman he had ever seen. This is delightful; and as I know it will not make you vain, I tell it to you.[14]

There was not a cloud in the midsummer sky when Robert

went to Bristol in July to make plans for the wedding in September; but on his return he wrote a desperate letter; subjecting his behavior while with his Priscilla to severe analysis, he felt that he had disgraced himself before her and her family by being jealous and unreasonable.

Now that I am at home and look back . . . on the events marking my stay in Bristol, I am ready to regret that which I have repeatedly done, to swear, deeply to curse myself for having so frequently enacted the part of a beastly brute to you while there. Indeed, indeed, my Lissy, I am filled with remorse for the many uneasy feelings my conduct towards you sometimes must have occasioned. I gave you reason to believe more than once that I doubted you or that my (love) to you was colder than it really was and a hundred things which have not until now struck me with the full force of the way which in every instance I did you. It is some satisfaction to me to know that you have seen me in my worst character in every respect, and this is the only spark of consolation which I have. I shall not be satisfied, dearest, my own dearest, until I receive a letter from you saying that you forgive me all my wicked ways to you. You will get this on Friday. Write by that day's mail to New Kent, C. H., New Kent City, Va., and let me see that you forgive me all the pain I now see I must have occasioned you.

If it will give you any pleasure to hear me say so, I now declare on my sacred *honor,* there is nothing, no one even in my own home in whom I place more unlimited confidence than in you. I think you nearer *perfection* than anything else on earth.

I have read your dear letters (three) which I found here over and over. They are exactly like you and, my God, how much better than I am—so kind, so loving. Indeed, my own dearest one, they typify your pure mind and noble heart. I will endeavor in time to make myself worthy of you. I will endeavor with all my heart and soul to do so. . . .[15]

Priscilla's answer to this letter must have been comforting; never again did he doubt her. Even when, a month later, in a panic for fear she could not be ready by September, she suggested postponing the date agreed upon, he did not seem unduly upset.

For God's sake, let me come to you as soon as possible. Each moment absent from you, my own dear, is a month, a year of time lapsed with you. By all means fix on the 12th. I shall expect you to do so, even earlier, the 9th. . . . I shall never miss the clothes or any preparation. I had as leave take you tomorrow with "calico dresses" than a month hence with all the finery in the world.[16]

He seemed increasingly sure of himself and of her love for him as the wedding day drew near:

You must not let Mary or anyone frighten you about being married. That ceremony which joins us together must be natural. We were born for each other. I have never felt the same sympathy or the slightest approach to it, for any other human being. I would not feel it for anyone else. As to your bad omens, construe them always in the opposite sense which they convey. They are, I have no doubt, auspicious signs. If being a devoted husband to you can make them so, most certainly this will be true. I think I should sooner face the realities of stabbing myself to the heart than of subjecting you to the slightest ill. Now that my love is formed, that I have tested you and know that I can't be deceived, nothing can shake me. I give you leave to try me after we are married.[17]

The parish record of St. James's Episcopal Church, which the Coopers regularly and devoutly attended, records the marriage as having taken place in Bristol, on September 12, 1839. John Tyler, Sr., was his son's best man; neither Jim Cooper nor Julia Fairlie Ogden could come, but at the very moment the ceremony took place Julia wrote to Priscilla:

"Oh, that I had the wings of a dove," how I would fly away to Bristol just to take a peep at the melancholy, mischievous, and merry things going on there. I try to picture to myself the manner in which you will behave on the "solemn occasion," but I can't for the life of me. Whether you will laugh or cry, or faint, or take it quietly and coolly—I can't imagine.

How much obliged I should be to one of the dear girls (if they are not too sad after it is all over) if they will take the trouble to write me an account of the wedding. . . .

God grant you may be as happy, dear Priscilla, as your noble, disinterested heart deserves to be.[18]

The bride and groom visited for a month at Woodlawn, the

plantation of Robert's eldest sister, Mary, and her husband, Mr. Jones; then they went home to Williamsburg. The Tylers had rented a large house, probably Bassett Hall, and Robert and his father had offices on the grounds. In her first letter to her loved ones in Bristol, Priscilla described the establishment and the members of the household very fully. Her letter is worth quoting in full, for it represents her at her best as a correspondent and gives information about the family into which she had married.

Williamsburg, Virginia
October, 1839

The bridal festivities so profusely extended to us in Charles City, that most hospitable of counties, ended last week. My honeymoon has waned, and I have at last settled down at home. If I can ever learn to think any place a home where my own dear father and sisters are not, I certainly can do so here, for a new father and mother have opened their arms and their hearts to me; new and lovely sisters cluster around me; and I am welcomed and approved of by any number of uncles, aunts, and cousins. The introduction to all of them was an awful ordeal to go through, you may be sure, but it is happily over, and I have now settled myself down absolutely as one of the family. I know you want me to tell you of each separate member, and of the house, and all my surroundings.

You know how entirely charming Mr. Tyler's father is, for you saw him at my wedding in Bristol, but you cannot imagine the tenderness and kindness with which he received me, his "new daughter," as he called me. Mr. Tyler's mother is very much as I imagined her from his description. She must have been very beautiful in her youth, for she is still beautiful now in her declining years and wretched health. Her skin is as smooth and soft as a baby's; she has sweet, loving black eyes, and her features are delicately moulded; besides this, her feet and hands are perfect; and she is gentle and graceful in her movements, with a most peculiar air of native refinement about everything she says and does. She is the most entirely unselfish person you can imagine. I do not believe she ever thinks of herself. Her whole thought and affections are wrapped up in her husband and children; and I thank God I am numbered with those dear children, and can partake with them in the blessing of her love. May He give me grace to be ever a kind and loving daughter to her.

The house is very large and very airy and pleasant, fronting on a large lawn and surrounded by a most beautiful garden. The parlor is comfortably furnished, and has that homelike and occupied look which is so nice. The prettiest thing in it, to my taste, though very old-fashioned, is the paper upon the walls, which depicts in half life-size pictures the adventures of Telemachus, on Calypso's enchanted isle. Telemachus is very handsome, Calypso and her nymphs are graceful as possible; and old Mentor as disagreeable and stern as all Mentors usually are. I find something new in the paper every day, and love to study it. The dining-room is opposite the parlor, across a broad passage, kept too bright and shiny almost to step upon, and is also a very spacious room, with a great deal of old family silver adorning the sideboard, and some good pictures upon the walls. There are two other rooms behind the parlor and the dining-room, one of which is used as a sitting and reading-room; for it is a large double house, flanked by offices in the yard, in which the library is kept, and one of which is used for law and business purposes by Mr. Tyler's father and himself.

The room in the main dwelling furthest removed and most retired is "the chamber," as the bedroom of the mistress of the house is always called in Virginia. This last, to say nothing of others, or of the kitchen, storerooms and pantries, is a most quiet and comfortable retreat, with an air of repose and sanctity about it; at least I feel it so, and often seek refuge here from the company, and beaux, and laughing and talking of the other parts of the house; for here Mother, with a smile of welcome on her sweet, calm face, is always found seated on her large arm-chair with a small stand by her side, which holds her Bible and her prayer-book—the only books she ever reads now—with her knitting usually in her hands, always ready to sympathize with me in any little homesickness which may disturb me, and to ask me questions about all you dear ones in Bristol, because she knows I want to talk about you. Notwithstanding her very delicate health, Mother attends to and regulates all the household affairs, and all so quietly that you can't tell when she does it. All the clothes for the children, and for the servants, are cut out under her immediate eye, and all the sewing is personally superintended by her. All the cake, jellies, custards, and we indulge largely in them, emanate from her, yet you see no confusion, hear no bustle, but only meet the agreeable result. . . .

All Mr. Tyler's sisters are lovely and sweet. Sister Mary—Mrs.

Jones, who is the oldest of all—I have already introduced to you in my letter from Charles City, where she resides, at "Woodlawn," one of the plantations, or "farms," as they are called here, of her husband, and where she so happily entertained us recently. Next comes Letitia, Mrs. Semple, married last February. She is very handsome and full of life and spirits. She has a place called "Cedar Hill," some distance from Williamsburg, in New Kent County, but is now here on a visit. Then comes Elizabeth, a very great belle here, though she is not yet seventeen. She is remarkably sweet and pretty, with beautiful eyes and complexion, and her hair curled down her neck. John, who is next to Mr. Tyler in age, and who was at my wedding, and therefore needs no description, is not here now, but he and his wife will spend next winter with his father, as he still attends the law department and higher scientific courses of "William and Mary" college, as it is termed in accordance with the original charter of King William and Queen Mary, although it is now and has been for many years a university. I have not seen her yet, but hear that she is very beautiful.

The two younger children, Alice and Tazewell, make up the family. . . . The children, with all the rest of the family seem very, very fond of me, but you must not suppose that all this affection and kindness make me vain. It is very comforting and sweet, but I know they all love me from no merit of my own, but from the devotion the whole family feel for Mr. Tyler, who is idolized by his parents, and profoundly loved and respected by his brothers and sisters.[19]

Priscilla's devotion to her new home and her husband's family was not so great that she would willingly miss Mary Grace's wedding to Frederic Sebastian Raoul. There are no letters describing the ceremony; and in the absence of any information except the entry in the church register at Bristol, we know only that it did take place in October. It was undoubtedly the occasion of great rejoicing, for the Raouls and the Coopers were bound to each other by close ties of affection, which had lasted for more than half a century.

Cooper had first known Mrs. Raoul, Mary Grace's new mother-in-law, as Caroline Eliza Theus Thompson, the widow of an invalid gentleman of means, who had left her an enormous plantation near Columbia, South Carolina. Her second husband, Jean

Rose Marie Desire Raoul de Champmanoir, was a romantic figure, an exiled Royalist, the intimate friend of King Louis XVI's nephew. De Champmanoir fled to America from Napoleon's wrath, was shipwrecked and brought ashore at Charleston. Being an able physician and a good man at business, he prospered there. When he was firmly enough established to take a wife, he married Caroline Eliza, and managed his own practice and her property so profitably that they grew rich.

In the early years of their marriage the couple entertained all visiting celebrities at their home in Columbia, and following his first visit there Cooper was a frequent visitor. The Raouls' friendship toward him had not wavered when the tide of his popularity turned. He had felt free to bring Mary Grace to visit them in 1831, as Mary Grace's journal indicates, and again in 1837, when she spent the better part of a year at Belleville, the country home not far from Columbia. It was probably on this latter occasion that she and Frederic fell in love. Both families were eager for the match. Caroline Eliza in 1839, the year of the marriage, bought the couple 1,200 acres near Mt. Meigs, Alabama, not far from Montgomery, and built them a spacious house, Longwood, near the estates on which her older children and her sister, Mrs. Lucas, were already established.[20] There was in the country round about a colony of transplanted Carolinians, attracted by the rumor that in Alabama a planter could live luxuriously at the cost of little effort by raising cotton with slave labor.

Like the capable young woman she was, Mary Grace attended to her duties as mistress of the place from the first as if she had always had to be responsible for the welfare of slaves and the happiness of a husband. She was already an experienced housekeeper; she soon learned to deal with emergencies in garden, dairy, poultry yard, and smokehouse.

Her young husband suited her exactly; his solid virtues contrasted most favorably with the shallow charms of the lover of long ago. That he did not impress Julia Fairlie Ogden when the newly married couple called on the family in New York would have mattered little to Mary Grace. Julia wrote to Priscilla shortly after the visit, saying that it was easy to see that Robert Tyler was made of finer stuff than Frederic.

> You ask me what I think of him. I like him very much. He reminds me of Jim—looks, manners, and everything. I must, however, confess myself disappointed in his beauty. From various little hints of Mary, profiles, etc., I expected a second Antinous. His figure is certainly fine, but that is all I can say for his personal appearance. But I like him because he seems so ingenuous. There is a sort of boyish freshness of feeling about him that I think very interesting. And then he does love Mary so entirely. I believe he thinks her perfection itself. And as to beauty, I am sure he thinks the Venus de Medici a fool to her.
>
> I don't think it was necessary for you to inform me that your husband was the more sensible. *Entre nous,* I am convinced in that particular, they are as different as vessels of delft and porcelain. The former may perhaps be the more useful vessel of the two, but who would not prefer the finer clay?[21]

With her usual discriminating taste Julia pronounced judgment on her favorite nieces' husbands, arriving at a fairly just estimate of both.

Young Mrs. Tyler was more than satisfied with her lot; she would not have changed places with any one in the world. In the intoxicating happiness of the early months of her married life she did not at all mind living with her husband's people. She loved them and found her new environment most stimulating. Williamsburg was a college town of about 1,500 inhabitants at this time, and was noted for its pleasant social atmosphere. The family enjoyed life there, for the years 1839-1840 were a peaceful interlude in John Tyler's stormy political career. He had resigned his seat in the Senate because of party discord and had not yet become involved in the presidential campaign of 1840, in which he was to be a candidate for the Vice-Presidency on the Whig ticket. At the moment, he was glad to have the opportunity to attend to his neglected law practice and to have leisure to devote to his invalid wife, his children, and his friends. Thomas Dew, president of the College of William and Mary, Judge N. Beverley Tucker, and Abel P. Upshaw were the cronies with whom he discussed politics; while the brilliant young men being trained at the college for leadership in the state supplied the younger members of the family with stimulating companionship. Priscilla wrote on April 28, 1840, to Mary Grace, that she had been the guest of honor at a dozen dinner parties and that she must go to a dozen more.

The Tylers belonged to the inner circle of the Tidewater aristocracy, for they had lived in and around Williamsburg since Henry Tyler I, a Cavalier escaping Puritan oppression in 1653, bought 250 acres of land in the vicinity. Williamsburg was built on the Tylers' middle plantation, the site for the Royal Governor's palace being bought from Henry Tyler II.[22] John Tyler II, Robert's father, and his father before him, John Tyler I, had taken a prominent part in Virginia politics; they felt, as did most Southerners of the upper class before the Civil War, that statesmanship was the only profession for a gentleman. Priscilla was not unprepared to understand the spirited political discussions that went on constantly among the Tyler men. She had heard her father argue as vehemently as did Robert and John Tyler, Senior and Junior; she liked such talk and occasionally contributed a level-headed suggestion. She hoped, however, that her husband would not go into public life, being eager for him to establish himself as a lawyer so that they might no longer than necessary be dependent on his father. In the meantime she minded very little being poor, for the future looked bright and the present was a love idyll.

She did not seem to cast a single backward glance at her career on the stage. It saddened her, of course, to hear how badly her father was doing without her, for he could not command an audience even in places like Montgomery, where he would not have accepted an engagement in the days of his greatness.

Mary Grace wrote to her of an appearance he made there in January, 1840:

I went to Montgomery and stayed two or three days . . . during which time we went to the theatre. We intended to have gone the week before and fixed upon our night, and chose our play, *Hamlet,* which Papa said he would play any night we elected. When the night came it rained and we could not go. . . . We had to put up the next week with *Damon and Pythias.* . . .

The play went off very well with the exception of a great dearth of supernumeraries. The . . . knaves that Damon stops to question were three, the soldiers that seized him in the senate house consisted of one, and the senators could not muster stronger than two, on the stage. There were vast numbers behind the scenes, to which Damon invariably addressed himself, not considering the visible gentry as sufficiently respectable in their appearance for his notice. No child—which cut up the scene with Hermione most terribly. With these exceptions, the play went off very well. Papa did his best, although it was his benefit and only thirty-seven dollars in the whole house. His voice was, as usual, perfect music compared with all around him.[23]

Greatly distressed by her sister's letter, but helpless for the time being to make satisfactory arrangements for Cooper, Priscilla busied herself with her husband's affairs. She helped him with his speeches, for he had an occasional case. "I write all the pathetic and romantic parts, and Mr. Tyler, the law and reason,"[24] she remarked to Mary Grace. She transcribed his verses, mended his shirts, and tried to economize by making her own clothes. Her "unhandywork," turned out badly; the dress she made reminded her of two French towns, "Too Long" and "Too Loose" (Toulon and Toulouse). Her letters are full of high spirits. She wrote to her brother, Jim, who was in Marietta, Georgia, one of the engineers in charge of the construction of the Western and Atlantic Railroad, teasing him about his love affairs. Like all happily married women, she had turned matchmaker, and hoped to interest him in Laura Towns, an old flame, or as an alternative, in Lizzie Tyler, her pretty sister-in-law.[25] Jim had plenty of initiative in such matters. He was at the time courting a Georgia girl, Fanny Spiers, and married soon after without consulting anyone. Mary Grace and Priscilla suffered a shock to their jealous affection, and disapproved of the match until they were convinced of Jim's happiness.

In August of 1840, Mr. and Mrs. Robert Tyler went to Bristol for what must have been a family conference. It was the first time since her marriage that her father and her husband had been under the same roof. Priscilla confided to Mary Grace that she found their behavior disconcerting:

Pa and Mr. Tyler agree about as much as oil and water. Pa really makes himself very disagreeable sometimes, especially in little short political opinions as he reads the newspapers. "The Whigs stand no more chance than a cat in hell without claws. Damn their bloods. They will cut their own damn throats." And such like little compliments, which I think in exceeding bad taste, to say the least, considering our being the candidates. Mr. Tyler bears it very well, generally giving one of his involuntary bursts of laughter.[26]

Robert and his father-in-law never resolved their differences of opinion about politics, but finally after much discussion the family came to agree that Cooper should quit the stage and sell the houses in Bristol. Jim had written that after he and Fanny were married he wanted his favorite among his younger sisters, Julia, to come to live with them in Marietta, near the work on which he was engaged. Olivia was to go to Mary Grace in Alabama; Ginny to be under the care of a friend in New York, where Julia Fairlie Ogden could keep an eye on her social career; Louisa was to be with Priscilla in Williamsburg until her father's plans were more settled.

The prospect of so many changes and of abandoning the well-loved home upset everyone. Melancholy, unusual to the Coopers, pervaded the household until there came a letter from Mary Grace that created a fever of excitement and rejoicing. Priscilla answered it immediately.

Bristol
August 20, 1840

Your letter has just arrived, my dearest sister, and diffused a general joy throughout the house. Thank God your troubles are now over. Your letter came just as Papa was starting for New York; so he cannot write today. He desires me to say everything for him. "Wish the dear child joy, etc., etc., etc." You never saw anything so pleased as he is. He could not eat a mouthful of breakfast and won't let any of us have the letter in our hands for more than half a second. And I heard him just now saying in soliloquy in his own room, "It is a d—d shame to crop the critter before it's half an hour old." Loo asked him for the lock of hair and he told her in the most imperative manner, he would see her in *hell* first, and I really think he would.

Loo wrote a letter to Aunt Julia informing her of it, but Pa refused to take it, saying Julia would see *his* letter and the *hair*. I suppose all New York will be favored with a peep.

Virginia disappeared immediately on hearing the news and has not since been heard of; so I suppose by this time the whole population are aware of *her* being an *aunt,* which she seems to consider the most important part of the event.

My feelings of joy, my dearest Mary, I cannot describe to you. I have been desponding upon every subject lately; consequently felt very uneasy about you. My mind was relieved of a weight of anxiety by your letter and I have done nothing but cry ever since. The dear little lock of hair. It is too sweet. The girls suspect you though of having sent a piece of Fred's whiskers instead of Tommy's hair. You must send me word as soon as possible all about him—the color of his eyes, size of his mouth, etc. Of course he enjoys the luxury of a straight nose.[27]

In so far as their delicacy had permitted, the two sisters had for months been exchanging confidences in regard to their symptoms, for Priscilla too was to have a child. She was overjoyed that all had gone well with Mary Grace, believing it a favorable augury that she would survive her own crisis. The Cooper family might be breaking up, but it was reassuring to know that there were no signs of its dying out.

As always when she was happy, Priscilla was full of fun. She called Mary Grace's attention to news from England's queen that might interest her.

I suppose you have heard that Victoria is expecting again. Poor thing! So much for not nursing! Louisa Victoria Adelaide Alexandria Leopoldina Maria Georgiana—the little princess royal. You had better send Tommy out to court her.[28]

Robert had made tentative plans to start practice in Petersburg after Priscilla's "ordeal" was over, but by the time little Mary Fairlie was born in December, 1840, he had been forced to abandon his own ambitions to help his father, who, to everyone's surprise, was named Vice-President on the Whig ticket.

Before John Tyler's nomination Priscilla had been in a flurry of preparation at the thought of her husband's establishing a law office in a town where they had friends and his prospects of success were good. By August, 1840, she was growing weary of dependence, as may be seen in a letter she wrote to Mary Grace.

At present the situation is anything but comfortable. Mr. Tyler has nothing to do scarcely in Williamsburg and his father won't send him away. The family are *very* extravagant. The governor pressed for money; consequently I never think of indulging in any little elegant superfluities, even to a yard of blue ribbon; in fact, never get a paper of pins without waiting a week or two to see if I *can* do without them. The governor is very generous though and has given me permission to have an account in every store in Williamsburg, which of course I do not avail myself of.[29]

Putting aside her own preference in the matter, since she was a reasonable woman and a loving wife, she yielded gracefully to necessity. She thought it seemed selfish in her to urge Robert to desert his father when John Tyler needed his son's services.

The baby made up for any inconvenience she suffered as an unwilling dependent in her father-in-law's home. She wrote volumes to Mary Grace and had from her volumes in return. They agreed that their charming infants must never meet; for they would be bound to fall in love at first sight, and everyone knew how unfortunate are the consequences of marriage between first cousins.

Having abandoned her determination that her husband begin his own career, she entered heart and soul into the excitement of the dramatic campaign of 1840. She wrote to everyone she knew, asking support of the Whig ticket. Her joy knew no bounds when Harrison and Tyler were swept into office by a high-pressure, steam-roller campaign.

The new President and Vice-President held differing opinions on every issue: Tyler was anti-national bank, anti-tariff, anti-distribution; and Harrison was pro on all these matters. This disagreement of the candidates had seemed to the Whigs when they made the ticket less important than the fact that Tyler was a states' rights man who would win Southern votes. Then too Harrison's nickname, *Tippecanoe,* rimed with *Tyler too* and made a good refrain.

"Van, Van
 Is a used up man!"

"With Tip and Tyler
 We'll bust Van's biler"

chanted the mob, who drank the party's free cider, enjoyed the free show and voted *against* Van Buren rather than *for* Harrison. Tyler's was an untenable position, teamed with a man whose opinions he could not share; however, he was not too much distressed. There seemed no reason why as Vice-President he could not continue his peaceful life in Williamsburg.

When at five o'clock on the morning of April 5, 1841, there was a knocking at the door, he must have been shocked by the thundering summons that awakened him from dreams. Daniel Webster's son, Fletcher, chief clerk in the State Department, and Mr. Beall, an officer of the Senate, had been sent to inform him of Harrison's death and that he was now President of the United States. He and his sons, Robert and John Tyler, Jr., left immediately and were in Washington the next morning.[30] The ladies of the household were to follow as soon as they could close the house in Williamsburg and assemble wardrobes in keeping with their new dignity as part of the family of the President of the United States.

6

WHITE HOUSE YEARS

1841-1844

WRITERS WHO describe Washington in 1841 say that it was not an imposing city, being composed of buildings widely scattered, separated from each other by vacant lots grown up in weeds. Charles Dickens scornfully called it "the city of magnificent intentions," and laughed at its stately avenues that "began in nothing and led nowhere," its public buildings that "had no public."[1] John Tyler's family came to the national capital in a less critical frame of mind than the great Englishman. They arrived in April when the flowers in the White House garden were blooming profusely. It was to be a hot and trying summer, but as yet the air was fresh and invigorating.[2] Although the White House was somewhat run-down and Congress in no hurry to appropriate funds for its rehabilitation, the Tylers found little fault with their accommodations. Priscilla wrote to her sisters that she thought her quarters luxurious, and felt no horror at her room's having been Harrison's death chamber. She was delighted with her clothes, especially "a pearl-colored silk that would set you crazy." Its effect "with pink roses in the hair and a *bouquet de corsage* of the same flowers" pleased her, as did "a white chip bonnet trimmed with moss rose buds," which she wore when she went calling.[3] Feeling rich because Robert had been given a position in the Land Office at $1,500 a year, she had bought herself and her baby daughter, Mary Fairlie, what she felt necessary to their new dignity. Robert's modest salary seemed affluence after the poverty of recent years; moreover, her father-in-law had promised that by November her father should be appointed military storekeeper at the arsenal in Frankford, with the pay and perquisites of a captain of infantry. This was the crowning blessing in all the good fortune that had recently come to Priscilla.

Shortly after the arrival of his family, the newly inaugurated President called his sons and daughters together and made them a little speech, begging them to remember that their position as the family of the chief executive was only temporary, that soon he would be plain John Tyler again. In the meantime they were to conduct themselves with proper humility.[4]

The Tylers without exception carried out faithfully the principles of social conduct outlined in this recommendation. John Tyler, inflexible in his political convictions, was to call forth from those who sought to change him bitter party recrimination; but he never let what was said in the Senate by a politician affect the welcome accorded a guest at the White House. He was an exception to the rule of hate that kept Benton and Clay, Jackson and Clay, Calhoun and Benton, Webster and Calhoun, at enmity.[5] Priscilla could not have been unaware of, and certainly she could not have been indifferent to, the fact that almost immediately political storms began to gather and to break on the President's head; but she preserved a judicious silence about these matters in her correspondence, and maintained before the world a cheerful disregard of the resentment which was called forth by John Tyler's every public act. In August of the first year (1841) he vetoed a bank bill sponsored by Clay. A crowd of hoodlums gathered outside the mansion, beating drums and blowing trumpets. They yelled, "Hurrah for Clay!" "A bank, a bank!" "Down with the veto!" The ladies of the house were frightened. When lights came on in the upstairs windows, the rowdies fled; but they came back the next night and burned the President in effigy.[6]

Behind this insult was a force more to be feared than mob spirit, for it was guided and directed by dangerous and able politicians. When the Whig leaders had added Tyler's name to the 1840 ticket they had anticipated no difficulty with the gentle Southerner, even though his professed beliefs ran counter to theirs on the proposed National Bank and on tariff. But when as President he stubbornly held to his opinions, they used every weapon available for the purpose of discrediting him. The malicious party press distorted everything he did into an offense; and the kindly, courteous man was made to seem to the public a monster. Hatred and abuse were visited upon him; he was called "an executive ass" and blamed by those who ridiculed him for every disagreeable happening, even an epidemic of influenza, called "Tyler's grippe."[7]

In September, 1841, the entire cabinet, with the exception of Webster, handed in their resignations; but the President's appointment of men more in sympathy with his principles did not end the discord. A martyr to his own consistency, he vetoed a Whig tariff bill the following June, and in the clamor which ensued he alienated Congress so completely that by July there was talk of impeachment. A man of Tyler's ability could have ridden the waves of public disapproval triumphantly by trimming his sails to the wind of opportunism; but the President was at the mercy of his own integrity as well as the enmity of those who hated him.

In view of these circumstances it was fortunate he possessed social intuition of a kind and degree that enabled him to avoid personal animosity, and it likewise was important that the official hostess of the White House be one who could match his own easy informality in everyday intercourse, his simple dignity on formal occasions. He asked Priscilla to act in this capacity, taking her consent for granted. It was obviously her duty to accept the responsibility since his wife was an invalid, and the two older Tyler girls, Mrs. Jones and Mrs. Semple, had establishments of their own which demanded their presence. Neither Lizzie Tyler, an inexperienced girl, nor Alice Tyler, a child, was capable of the tedious routine of presiding at bi-weekly receptions, tri-weekly dinners, monthly public levees, and entertainment of the callers who every night crowded the Green Room. The warm friendship between Elizabeth and Priscilla precluded any sense of rivalry in regard to rank. They shared the social obligations from the spring of 1841 until February of 1842, when Elizabeth was married. They were devoted to each other, and all Washington was pleased to see, out walking on a pleasant day, charming Mrs. Robert Tyler and pretty Miss Tyler, with little Mary Fairlie between them, clinging to her mother's hand. When during the summer the gardens of the White House were opened two evenings a week for a public concert by the Marine band, the President sat on the south porch, his daughter and daughter-in-law on either side, as delighted with the sunset and the gentle evening breeze as were the passers-by with their amiable courtesy. When there was a reception of all the school children, Elizabeth and Priscilla received together. "Nothing," said the discriminating Mrs. Ellet in commenting on the Washington social world, "could surpass the quiet and unaffected grace with which the ladies received and acknowledged the courtesies of all who paid their respects."[8]

Occasionally Mrs. Semple or Mrs. Jones, the elder daughters, would relieve Priscilla temporarily, but from April of 1841 to March of 1844 the strenuous program of social activities revolved largely around her. She had very little time to spend with her father, and felt that she neglected her husband, her baby, and her invalid mother-in-law. Life in the White House was a relentless succession of entertainments, a ceaseless round of paying social calls.

Though Priscilla found her duties arduous, she found them in a sense rewarding. She tried very hard to please John Tyler. Fortunately she had from the first a wise friend to whom to turn for help. When in doubt whether or not to leave cards in person at the homes of those who paid their respects at the President's mansion, she asked Mrs. Madison's advice. "Return all your visits by all means," decreed that arbiter of elegance—herself very kind and inelegant.[9] Dolly—a strange sight in her remarkable turban—painted, powdered, and dipped snuff; but no one knew better than she how to make herself liked. Priscilla would have been lost without this jolly, buxom dame, for every day presented problems baffling to her inexperience. Mrs. Madison was in and out of the White House like a good neighbor, and her presence was always reassuring. All the Tylers regarded her as a kind friend and found her an invaluable asset at public functions, for she had a smile and a ready word for everyone.

John Tyler, too, had his virtues as a social solvent. Priscilla, standing by his side at a levee or reception, tried to approximate his unpretentious courtesy and consideration of those about him. After having heard him talk to all manner of people, she wrote her sisters that she thought his powers as a conversationalist were not surpassed or even equalled by those of any of the great men in Washington.[10]

Strangely enough, among the distinguished group of cabinet members and officials with whom she was thrown, Priscilla chose the awe-inspiring Daniel Webster as her favorite. It was generally agreed that no one could be as great as he looked. "Like a cathedral in britches" one admirer declared him to be. Most people were tongue-tied in his presence, but he and she entertained each other with "enchanting nonsense" and "delightful gossip."[11]

As the Secretary of State, he usually took her in to the cabinet dinners and sat upon her right. She felt awkward at these gatherings—for she was the only woman present—and would have found them tedious except that her majestic friend unbent and devoted his considerable powers to making himself charming. He looked after her comfort in little ways, telling her which wines to drink and pointing out the food she was most likely to enjoy. The first time she faced the long table, with all the flowers and candles, and the crowd of brilliantly dressed diplomats, bedecked with glittering orders, it was too much for her. She described the occasion to her sisters in a letter, dated May, 1841.

. . . We have had a Cabinet dinner, and I have disgraced myself with Father forever. Just in the full tide of successful experiment, at the moment the ices were being put upon the table, everybody in good humor, and all going "merry as a marriage bell," what should I do but grow deathly pale, and, for the first time in my life, fall back in a fainting fit! Mr. Webster, who was sitting next me, picked me up in his arms, and took me away from the table; and Mr. Tyler, with his usual impetuosity, deluged us both with ice-water, ruining my lovely new dress, and, I am afraid, producing a decided coolness between himself and the Secretary of State. I had to be taken to my room, and poor Mr. Webster had to be shaken off, dried and brushed, before he could resume his place at the table![12]

Seasoned actress she might be, but she experienced considerable stage-fright at being called upon to appear before such an audience. After a short time she became more accustomed to her stellar role and pleased the President and amazed herself by performing her duties with what seemed easy grace. She wrote to Mary Grace in April, declaring that she actually felt at home in the White House.

What wonderful changes take place, my dearest Mary! Here am I, *nee* Priscilla Cooper (*nez retrousse,*[13] you will perhaps think), actually living in, and—what is more—presiding at, the White House! I look at myself like the little old woman, and exclaim: "Can this be I?" I have not had one moment to myself since my arrival, and the most extraordinary thing is that I feel as if I had been used to living here always; and receive the Cabinet, ministers, the Diplomatique Corps, the heads of the army and navy, etc., etc., with a facility which astonishes me. "Some achieve greatness—some are born to it." I am plainly born to it. I really do possess a degree of modest assurance that surprises me more than it does any one else. I am complimented on every side; my hidden virtues are coming out. I am considered "charmante" by the Frenchmen, "lovely" by the Americans, and "really quite nice, you know," by the English. . . .[14]

Loudly protesting to her family her complete self-assurance, she was in reality walking warily among the dangers that preeminence is heir to; but by taking the President as her model and choosing wise advisers like Dolly Madison and Webster, she managed adroitly to disarm the enemies of the administration and appeal to humble folk as well. A butcher who dined with the Tylers said he never felt more at home in his life.[15] De Bacourt, the

French minister—self-revealed in his memoirs as the most objectionable of snobs—spoke disparagingly of Webster as "pompous" and of Clay as a "farmer."[16] Before he met Mrs. Tyler he sneered that this is a singular country, for in the United States a woman can pass from the boards of a theatre to what "serves as a Republican throne."[17] After he had dined with Priscilla at General Macomb's, he still did not see why everyone praised her beauty and her matchless elegance, for she seemed to him simple and childlike. He writes that she says "little things which are rather amusing" and repeats at length their talk at dinner, in which he completely outshines her as a conversationalist. Priscilla seems to have made him comfortable by catering shamelessly to his vanity. The supercilious gentleman admired nothing in America except Niagara Falls and the Hudson River; however, his account of the evening with Mrs. Tyler ends by his grudgingly admitting that she has proved to be "a little woman who seems a good fellow."[18]

For all the apparent poise with which Priscilla dealt with disagreeable people like de Bacourt, this encounter must have cost an effort. Good taste, common sense, and breeding sometimes break down under strain, and her self-control is to be applauded. She might have told this patronizing foreigner of a Frenchman greater than he, Prince Talleyrand, who had been her grandparents' intimate friend, or of Joseph Bonaparte, twice a king, on whose knee she had sat as a child, when he came—as he often did—to visit her father.

De Bacourt was obnoxiously in evidence during the long visit paid in Washington by the Prince de Joinville, a son of Louis Philippe. The young aristocrat had been to America during the administration of Van Buren and had refused official invitations with considerable disregard of diplomatic conventions. He had orders from his royal father to conduct himself differently on this trip, and was on his good behavior when he arrived in Washington in October of 1841.

The Tylers had brought with them from Williamsburg all their servants, trained to look after guests in the best Virginia tradition. Since their arrival in Washington, the family had done a great deal of informal entertaining. Decanters stood on the sideboard of the White House just as they had at their former home, and no guest ever entered the doors without being welcomed warmly and offered refreshment. The regular dinners, levees, and receptions occasioned no great strain on their domestic economy, but entertainment appropriate for royalty was a different matter. For a number of reasons they felt themselves at a loss. Out of spite Congress had refused to grant Tyler the usual sum appropriated for upkeep of the White House. For lights, fuel, and such expenses the President, not a rich man, paid out of his own pocket.[19] There was a very limited budget for entertainment. Priscilla appealed to Mrs. Semple, who generously left her own household problems to help her favorite sister-in-law. The Tylers felt tender concern for Priscilla's health at this time, for she was to bear her second child in the spring and was not well. It was good to have the elder woman's help in the preparations to be made for the dinner to which the cabinet, the foreign ministers, the high ranking officers of the Army and Navy came, bringing their wives. Afterwards there was a huge reception which de Bacourt thought "ridiculous and tiresome." He remarked, "Happily the Prince with his natural gayety amused himself with the strange toilettes of the women and bore with great patience the indiscretion of all who asked to be presented, all the familiarity of their manners and language."[20]

In spite of the behavior of the guest of honor, this affair, the most important social event in 1841, passed off well, establishing yet more firmly the favorable impression Tyler and his pretty daughters made at every public function. It seemed that socially they could do no wrong; whereas politically the President could do nothing to please his captious critics.

Priscilla kept a journal for the first five weeks of 1842, the second year of the Tyler administration. The handsomely bound book in which it is written she left to her eldest daughter when she died. She cared little for possessions and believed, as she once said, in going through life with "a light field equipment";

so if she had not prized her diary, she would have mislaid it or thrown it away. Certainly, however, she did not hold as sacred this record of her days of greatness. Some child has filled pages of it with crude drawings; and Priscilla herself has scribbled in it a remarkable miscellany: recipes, most of them as extravagant as one that begins: "Take a dozen eggs and a quart of cream . . ."; laundry lists; poems written by various members of the family; personal memoranda; first drafts of letters. The diary proper covers only a few pages but is most interesting in that it represents what she really thought far better than her conversations with visitors or her correspondence addressed to Mary Grace and her other sisters. Checked against her letters, it suggests that even when she wrote to the family she edited what she told them, ruling out what seemed to her ill-advised.

In the entry of January 1, describing a reception given on New Year's Day, she speaks of the Russian minister's looking "unusually hideous" in his beautiful uniform, of the "sovereign people" as a mob, of not seeing a single "intelligent looking" person except Calhoun and Webster.[21] To be sure, the letter which deals with the same occasion refers to Mr. Fox, the Minister from Great Britain, as being a "perfect bat," and describes Mrs. Bodisco, the Russian Minister's wife, as looking like a pretty milkmaid. However, the severity of her criticism is considerably toned down and the account of the party as a whole considerably toned up. In the following report of the affair it seems an enjoyable occasion.

The 1st of January, 1842, is past, never to return, and I am nearly on the point of going off with it. I never felt so tired in all my life as I am this evening, standing up for three hours and shaking hands with I don't know how many thousand people—such big fists as some of the people had, and such hearty shakes as they gave my poor little hand, too! One great hearty countryman gave me a clutch and a shake I almost expired under; but I could not help laughing when Fletcher Webster whispered to me: "When taken to be well shaken." At half past eleven we ladies took our station at the upper end of the Blue Room, while Father stood in the centre (we being the lesser lights), to receive the foreign ministers and the Cabinet, who made their appearance half an hour before the crowd. This first half an hour was a very pleasant one, and passed rapidly away. The Diplomatique Corps were all present but Mr. Fox, who sent an apology, pleading indisposition. He is a complete *bat,* only making his appearance by candlelight. The costumes of the foreign ministers were very beautiful, and as each entered, surrounded by his attaches, the scene was quite imposing. The Baron de Roenne is peculiarly soldierlike and noble in his appearance; and there is a simplicity and quietude in his whole bearing and conversation that to me is peculiarly agreeable. Mr. Bodisco and his beautiful wife came later than the rest. She is rather of the milk-maid order of beauty. I can imagine her dropping a courtesy like the maid in the song, with, "My face is my fortune, sir, she said;" and her face really has been her fortune as regards a fine house, fine carriage, and fine clothes—and a fine husband, too, for the matter of that, for nothing could be finer than Mr. Bodisco's uniform. It is perfectly dazzling in its magnificence, his whole breast glittering with orders. At twelve o'clock the crowd rushed in — men, women, and children—a very orderly crowd, though, and nicely dressed. A little after the first rush of the "sovereign people" came the ladies and their respective escorts. I cannot say who I thought the prettiest woman—perhaps it was Mrs. Potts, Mr. Rose's sister; she is very lovely looking.[22]

The Bodiscos gave a great ball on January 4, and in describing it Priscilla added to their portraits a few finishing touches. Since the extract is from the diary, it is quite merciless in its realism.

Well, the great party is over, and a poorer affair, considering all the talk about it, I never saw. It was one solid body. As to moving about and seeing who was there and how they were dressed, that was impossible. Bodisco was more like a head servant than master of his own house. Jumpy as can be, he was busy arranging lamps, seeing about refreshments, seeing about champagne, etc., etc., during the whole evening. Young Nicholas, aged eight months, was up at two o'clock dressed in blue silk covered with white muslin. He looked ridiculous. Every room in the house was thrown open, including the bedroom of Bodisco himself. His bed appeared in all grandeur, covered with a green satin coverlet with pillow slips to match. Madame was magnificently attired in pink satin and lace, splendid diamonds. I really envied them, not for their luster but for their value. Mary Fairlie's education might be purchased by them. I feel very fatigued today from my last night's exertion, as well as having spent the morning writing letters of invitation to the Diplomatic Corps who dine with us on the fifteenth. I dread the day, for I know it will be stupid to them. How very, very much I regret my ignorance of French. It would be all important to me now. Tonight is the assembly night.[23]

There are in her private record many other comments on the great and the near great who were entertained at the White House. Lord Morpeth, the future Earl of Carlisle, fared no better than the rest, though all the blood of the Howards flowed in his noble veins. "His face is red; his hair is light; his manner awkward," Priscilla commented, and declared he sat by her side for three hours without making a remark worth remembering.[24] She qualified her disapproval by saying she hears he is a good democrat, "which is a high recommendation in an Englishman and a nobleman."

Mrs. Tyler, whom de Bacourt thought too sweet to be interesting, expressed none of these opinions openly. Nor did she seem to outsiders to be concerned over the ceaseless bickering between Whigs and Democrats; nevertheless, she includes in the diary an excellent account of an exchange of insult between Wise and Adams on the floor of the House, which shows that she was entirely at home in the visitors' gallery of the Capitol, and might have commented astutely on the political scene had not prudence sealed her lips.[25]

On February 10 she decided to abandon her diary; she wearied of writing what seemed to her "chronicles of idleness and folly." Her temporary disenchantment with the Washington social merry-go-round, attributable to the discomfort of her pregnancy, made her in love with domesticity. She cherished the brief moments of freedom she found to devote to her husband and child, to her mother-in-law, to visiting with Sophie Bache, a friend from Bristol days who was living in Washington.

She always was deeply moved when people spoke to her of the greatness of her father or the charm of her mother. There is in her journal an entry that is quite touching. She was chatting with Samuel L. Southard, the president of the Senate, in an assembly room which had been the old theatre. He told her of having witnessed there "the finest acting possible for the mind of man to conceive." He had sat by John Adams, who agreed with him that the actor was better than John Kemble, Talma, Cooke, Kean or Macready—all of whom they had both seen.

Priscilla wrote, "Though my heart told me to whom he alluded, I could not help asking what was the play and who was the actor."

"The play was *Macbeth;* the performer, Mr. Cooper," answered Southard.

Priscilla went on to say that she could not control her emotion at this praise. "I looked around too and thought that not only Papa had trod these boards. . . . I looked at the velvet dress of Mrs. Tyler and thought of the one I wore as Lady M. seven years before, when we struggled through a miserable engagement of six nights of bad weather, bad houses, and bad spirits. The little money we did earn was never paid."[26]

Priscilla had identified herself with her husband's people, as every good wife tries to do; however, it must have afforded her satisfaction for the Tylers and the rest of the world to see her on familiar terms with Washington Irving, recently appointed Minister to Spain. He came to Washington in March of 1842 at the invitation of the President and let everyone know that he was as much impressed by the fact that she was the daughter of Tom and Mary Fairlie Cooper as by her position as official hostess at the White House.

She was far from well, but in spite of her approaching confinement she enjoyed his visit and that of Charles Dickens, who shared the honors of the White House hospitality.

New York had entertained the great English novelist lavishly with balls, tableaux taken from his books, banquets, and every kind of complimentary attention. It was hardly possible to top such display, but "Boz" was favorably impressed by his host and hostess; and when he wrote his *American Notes,* he tempered his sharp wit in giving his impressions of them. He spoke of Mrs.

Robert Tyler as "a very interesting, graceful and accomplished lady,"[27] and of the President as "becoming his station singularly well."[28]

Even so, Dickens's behavior, as described by the New York *Herald,* suggests that he was somewhat bored on the evening he and Irving were the guests of honor at a public reception.

When it was understood that there would be a levee and that Irving and Dickens would both be there, the rush was tremendous. It was as much as the police officers could do to keep the passages open. Even the circle usually left around the Chief Magistrate was narrowed to almost nothing by the pressure. It was computed that the East Room alone contained upward of 3,000 persons.

There was one point of interest: Washington Irving and the lady who presided on this occasion with surprising courteousness and grace—Mrs. Robert Tyler. Irving, now grown more fat than "bard beseems" is yet distinguished by that glow of genius and humor in his eye, and smile and utterance which make him the adored of the N. Y. world of fashion. . . .

Who is that lady receiving such homage from the new Ambassador? She is the player's daughter, but she is a President's daughter, and she is welcoming from her elevation her mother's friend of bygone years. . . . Ought there not to be almost as much interest for an American in these associations as in the presence of Boz? . . . Boz retired after an hour's exhibition, bequeathing all the unused literary enthusiasm to be poured on Washington Irving. . . .[29]

Priscilla confided to her sisters her impressions of the two guests, when on another occasion they dined informally at the White House. Her obvious preference for Irving suggests a pardonable bias of opinion.

I cannot tell you anything about Boz we have not seen in the papers. I was determined to see him, which I did, in spite of my indisposition. I have seen him twice, once in the morning when he called, and then again at the levee in the evening.

He is not at all romantic looking, is rather thick set, and wears entirely too much jewelry, very English in his appearance, and not the best English. He was accompanied by his wife, quite a sweet-looking, plump woman, tastelessly dressed, and more

English looking than Boz himself. Poor fellow, he seemed horribly bored by the crowd pressing around.

What think you . . . he and Washington Irving were both speaking to me at the same time. I am charmed with Washington Irving. He took me in to the dinner Father gave for me, and he talked to me of Mama all the time, telling me a great many anecdotes of Grandmama's home and surroundings in the old times.[30]

Of greater national importance, though of less personal interest to her, was Lord Ashburton's arrival on June 12, 1842, to negotiate for a peaceful settlement of the dispute in regard to the boundary line between Canada and the United States—a mission upon the outcome of which depended, some thought, peace between the two countries. Such an occasion called for a reception worthy of the important guest. John Adams, that tart critic, said the distinguished visitor was treated "in royal fashion." "The courtesies of the President and Mrs. Robert Tyler were all that the most accomplished European court could have displayed."[31] This was praise indeed, coming as it did from a man who knew the capitals of Europe and was never ready with a compliment.

The private life of Priscilla in 1842 was no less crowded with events than her public career as official hostess for the President. Three weddings, a birth, and a death followed each other so closely that there was little time for rejoicing on which sorrow did not obtrude. She was in Bristol for a short time in the summer of that year for the wedding of her sister Julia to Allan Campbell. The bride and groom had met the previous February, when Julia Cooper had gone to visit her brother, Jim, in the wilds of Georgia. Among the rough engineers in the construction camp where Jim and his wife, Frances, were living was a man who would have looked distinguished in any group. He was tall and handsome and came honestly by his air of breeding, for he was from an excellent family in upstate New York. The young people, being on alien soil and a little lonely, were attracted to each other.

Julia recorded in her diary the progress of a courtship that might have been conducted under the eye of Queen Victoria herself, it was so proper and followed so faithfully the conventions of the nineteenth century. First Allan Campbell called; then he brought a keepsake annual, Heath's *Book of Beauty;* well chaperoned they went walking and riding. After a series of delicate attentions, he proposed to her against the backdrop of a beautiful view; but they waited to be really engaged until Julia's father had given his sanction. This he did most readily; in fact, the whole family rejoiced at Julia's good fortune.[32]

Shortly afterward from Mary Grace in Alabama came the news of Olivia Cooper's engagement to Dr. Alfred McDonald, a young physician who had recently opened an office in Mt. Meigs. He too was an eminently eligible man, and the elder sisters were proud that the penniless younger Cooper girls were able with little family backing to find good husbands. Only Virginia and Louisa were still dependent upon their father, who with a good salary as keeper of the arsenal at Frankford should have been able to provide for them. Since he would not—or could not—be economical, Priscilla tried to help him by having Louisa for long visits at the White House, and Julia Fairlie Ogden kept Virginia with her in New York.

Priscilla was as much devoted to Elizabeth Tyler, Robert's sister, as to her own family, and was delighted when her romance with William Waller of Williamsburg turned out happily.

"All smiles and dimples," Lizzie was wed February 7, 1842. "She conducted herself well and looked very pretty," Priscilla wrote in her diary. It was a quiet wedding; only Mrs. Madison, the members of the Cabinet, and the intimate friends, known as "the Corporal's Guard," attended. When one of the guests expressed surprise that the bride seemed happy to give up the gayety of Washington for life in a country town, Mr. Webster in his resonant voice quoted lines from Scott's *The Lay of the Last Minstrel:*

> "Love rules the court, the camp, the grove,
> And love is heaven; and heaven is love."

Priscilla beamed at Mr. Webster. It seemed to her that he always said the right thing most eloquently at the right time.

Lizzie's wedding and the reception afterwards was the only

public occasion in Washington at which the elder Mrs. Tyler appeared. Generally she stayed in her room, an invalid, avoiding excitement of any kind; but that night, beautifully dressed, she had come to do honor to the bride and groom. Her devoted daughter-in-law, Priscilla, thought her the most distinguished woman in the room and the most charming—"completely self-forgetful in her desire to make others happy."[33]

Priscilla's second child was born that spring, and Mrs. John Tyler was deeply gratified that the baby was christened Letitia Christian in her honor. By that time there was no escaping the realization that the invalid could live only a little longer. Sadness lay like a shadow upon the household. Her husband, who loved her dearly, felt his emotions strained to the breaking point by personal grief and the unhappy turn of his political fortunes. He buried himself in work. Rising with the sun, he stayed at his desk without a break until three-thirty in the afternoon, at which time the family dined together. After candle light he interviewed visitors and performed miscellaneous social chores until bedtime at ten o'clock.[34] Priscilla deliberately broke in upon this exhausting routine one morning and brought him hurrying from his office in answer to a message that Mrs. Madison was in the drawing room and must see him immediately on important business. She had dressed little Mary Fairlie as a miniature Dolly in turban, shawl, paint and patches, and had coached her in a good-natured imitation of that lady's speech and manner. John Tyler was delighted by this prank and laughed heartily enough to relax temporarily the tensions which impending tragedy and public disapproval had imposed upon him.[35]

Mrs. Tyler's death occurred in September. Priscilla had gone with the children for a brief visit to Brooklyn. Letitia Tyler, knowing herself to be dying, sent Robert to bring them home. They arrived too late. "My poor husband suffered dreadfully when he was told that Mother's eyes were constantly turned to the door watching for him," Priscilla wrote. "Nothing can exceed the loneliness of this large and gloomy mansion—hung with black—its walls echoing our sighs. . . ."[36]

During the month of mourning which followed, the hostile press was silent and Tyler's opponents in the political arena showed respect for his bereavement. The animosity of the Whigs had more or less exhausted itself during the first years of his administration in the protests that greeted his vetoes. His remaining years as President were to be comparatively free from persecution by his enemies.

This fact may be partly responsible for the change of mood noticeable in the happier tone of the letters Priscilla wrote in 1843. Now completely recovered from the birth of the baby, Letitia, she seemed to put aside the melancholy induced by the pain and sorrow of the year just past. She inaugurated 1843 by celebrating Mary Fairlie's third birthday with a most elaborate costume party. The honoree was dressed as a fairy, with a wand and wings and a diamond-starred crown; her baby sister was a little Dutch girl. The daughter of the Spanish minister in embroidered satin and diamonds represented a princess of her own country. A son of the New York Schermerhorns came as a Greek boy. There were turbaned Turks and veiled Sultanas, tiny brigands generously bewhiskered, all kinds and conditions of small-scale men and women. Mrs. Madison was the only grown-up invited, but Cabinet officers, diplomats, and Supreme Court judges came to look on. Warring politicians forgot their differences as they watched the children, and everyone agreed that it was a successful occasion. Martin, the White House doorkeeper, is reported to have said, "There is more innocence in that room than ever was there before or ever will be again until we have another children's party."[37]

It was good for the family to have the silence of death exorcised by the laughter of children. The White House must have seemed a more cheerful place for days afterwards.

Priscilla herself had undergone a remarkable change. She approached her official duties in high good humor. Copied in her journal is the first draft of a letter (undated) in which she described to her sisters her meeting with Napoleon's famous aide de camp, Count Henri Bertrand, Grand Marshal of the court.

You say you hear Bertrand is coming to this country. My dear, he has come, seen, and conquered—or he has come, been seen, and I have been conquered. The Marshal arrived during the President's absence in Virginia, and the whole duty of entertaining him fell upon me. To be sure, Mr. Tyler is here, but he is only Prince Consort. Of course I was equal to the situation. He arrived on Saturday evening, and sent me word asking at what hour I could see him, and at what hour he might call. I appointed eight o'clock, it being then seven. I immediately sent for the officers of the Cabinet and was surrounded by them when the old hero arrived, accompanied by his suite. He bowed to the very ground, and I curtseyed quite as low. I cannot convey to you any idea of how charmingly I received him. The hour that he spent, he spent in complimenting me in French and English rather jumbled together, while I returned his compliments in the same eccentric mixture of languages.

At last, after a flourishing speech and squeezing my hand, with a second low bow over it, he departed, followed by his suite, each giving a profound obeisance. I could not resist the impulse, and as the last mustachioed Frenchman left the room, I turned a pirouette on one foot, and then dropping a low curtsey, said I begged the cabinet's pardon; whereat Mr. Tyler was exceedingly wrathy, though everyone else said it was the sweetest thing I had done all evening.

The Marshal was to leave the next morning, Sunday, but I sent him an invitation for Monday evening. You should see the note of acceptance he wrote. I have it in my book of autographs. He had intended leaving, but my gracious invitation was not to be resisted. I had such a short time to accomplish a great deal, but, my usual administrative powers called into activity, I succeeded in doing all I wished to do: sent out two hundred invitations to the *creme de la creme* of Washington society.

At eight o'clock the party was assembled, formed of the very prettiest girls and the nicest people I could collect. All the officers of the army and navy appeared in their uniforms, the diplomatic corps in full court costume. I stood at the head of the blue center room near the window. As the Marshal arrived and walked through the hall, the band struck up the Marseillaise. The guests fell back on either side of the end of the room, leaving a wide path for Bertrand to advance to where Josephine—I mean, I—stood surrounded by the Cabinet. To describe the reverences he made, followed by his son and each of his suite in turn would be vain. I returned them with Grandmama's old-fashioned curtseys, such as must have existed in the days of the Empire. Soon after his arrival the band struck up for dancing. I only danced twice—once to open the ball with Count Bertrand, the Marshal's son, and once again with his Aide de Camp, at his request . . . two young Frenchmen composed entirely of pantaloons and mustaches.

For the rest of the evening my guests demanded my attention. No party ever went off better. Father with his usual kindness had given me *carte blanche* before he left. My supper was splendid. (It is so easy to entertain at other people's expense.) The prettiest things on the table were the pyramids of pomegranates with their skins peeled off and the Malaga grapes. They looked like rubies and emeralds. I had quantities of flowers in vases down the tables, and festoons of grapes growing from vase to vase the whole length of the table. The table was covered, of course, with everything in the way of jellies, ice creams, and quantities of the most beautiful French bon-bons. Nothing was on the long principal table but things of the most aerial, glittering description. Meats of all descriptions were banished to the side tables; and altogether everything was as plentiful and brilliant as I could make it. I personally directed everything. When the Marshal led me in to supper, he seemed completely overcome, and putting his hand over his heart, said, "Ah, madame . . . all zis for me?"

The only *contretemps* that occurred was that I gave him with a sweet smile a most splendid-looking sugar plum without looking at the picture on it, which I afterwards discovered to my horror to be that of an ape.

The old gentleman did not leave until all the guests had departed, and then made a long speech of adieu, saying at the end, "I zink vous etes charmante, madame . . . I zink you one vary good woman . . . and all your people must lof you. Adieu. Madame, I shall never forget you."

Then saluting my hand in the most chivalrous, French, respectful, delicious manner, he left me alone in my glory.

I looked very well for me. I was dressed in a rose-colored satin trimmed in blonde lace flowers and a charming head dress of white bugles on my head.[38]

It was in the summer of 1843 that the President took the Robert Tylers with him on an official journey to Boston; there the dedication of the Bunker Hill Monument was to take place,

June 17. On the way they stopped at Baltimore, where they were welcomed by cheering crowds and were given a banquet and a reception. They were pleasantly surprised by the warmth with which they were received in Philadelphia and New York, in which latter city 400,000 people turned out and 10,000 troops. The trip was a steady progress of triumph until they reached Boston —a place not much given to wild enthusiasm. Priscilla's letter to her brother-in-law, Frederic Raoul, describing their travels makes light of the infirmities which prevented her from attending many of the festivities, and caused her to miss Webster's speech, which, it was predicted, would last as long as the monument.

Here I am, my dear Fred, in the land of steady habits; and as today is Sunday and I am forbidden to go to church, I will write to you. I wrote to Mary a month ago. She has treated my letter with silent contempt. I will try to see if I can get anything better out of you—her lord and master.

I am the most unfortunate person in the world. I started from Philadelphia with the President to come to Boston to the Bunker Hill oration and have missed all the most delightful parts of the town in the following manner. On board the steam boat coming from Philadelphia I ran with all force against an iron bar, which hit me upon the top of my head and caused loss of all sensation and afterwards very disagreeable sensations.

When we got to Princeton I was so ill that I had to be medicined, put in a warm bath, and finally have an immense mustard plaster put on the back of my neck, with which plaster on I went to sleep! Slept one hour, and woke to find myself with a blister on my neck a square foot in size, just above my dress.

The President and suite spent a day in Princeton, partaking of every sort of charming festivity; and I had to stay in bed. In New York all my pleasure was marred by the same thing. My blister was irritating and painful. I became better the day before I left, but on board the steamboat coming here I went to bed feeling quite well and woke in the morning with a face swelled out about a foot. I arrived here in that situation—had leeches applied immediately, went to bed, and have actually just arisen from it—having missed the oration for which I came expressly.

Such an ugly disfigured wretch as I am, you cannot imagine. Wanting to look my very best, I look like the old boy himself. . . .

I would have given anything could you and Mary have been with us this summer on our trip; such a triumphal passage as we have had I never could have imagined. When we arrived in New York there were four hundred thousand people assembled to greet us. You see, I won't allow it was only for the President. The bay was crowded with boats of every description. Seventy-four men-of-war down to thousands of club boats. The yards of the ships were all manned and cannons going off in every direction. The colors were flying from every ship in the harbor, bands of music were playing, and ten thousand troops stationed round the Battery. I never saw so magnificent a spectacle in my life. All the other cities had done their best, but none have the number of inhabitants or the natural advantages of New York. The President had really showers of bouquets and wreaths thrown upon him everywhere. Windows of the houses have been filled with the most beautiful women waving their handkerchiefs and casting flowers in his path. These latter demonstrations Mr. Tyler takes as intended solely for himself.

In Princeton, Father was met by twenty-six of the most beautiful girls I ever saw, dressed in white, with wreaths of flowers on their heads. They bore with them a long line of flowers, reaching from one end of the group to the other, as thick as my body, all of the choicest kind. This was presented with a very pretty little speech, which Father answered most charmingly. After the young ladies were disposed of, we were all placed in barouches drawn by six horses, and accompanied by forty young collegians—each mounted upon one of Capt. Stockton's splendid race horses. A troop of soldiers followed and a troop preceded us with bands of martial music. We arrived at the Captain's residence where we remained a day and a night. I have sent you a paper describing all the various receptions. . . .

I am beginning to feel quite conceited and *grand* with all the fuss that is being made about us. Mr. Tyler makes a speech to-night to the Repealers, by invitation of a delegation.

Goodnight, my dearest brother. I very often think of you and of all your numerous acts of kindness towards me while with you. You cannot imagine with what pleasure I look back to my visit to Alabama.[39]

Tyler and his suite made a favorable impression in all the cities in which they appeared. "Especially popular was Mrs. Robert Tyler, whose attractiveness," Mr. Chitwood says in his biography of John Tyler, "was noted by more than one reporter."[40]

Among the few things Priscilla kept through the years was a clipping (undated) from *The True Sun,* a New York paper, which on this occasion had flattering things to say about her presence in the President's party.

MRS. ROBERT TYLER

The publicity which has been given to the names of the ladies in the President's suite is our apology for alluding to Mrs. Robert Tyler, his very interesting and lovely daughter-in-law. She is the child of Mr. Cooper, the tragedian, and the late celebrated belle, Miss Fairlie, of this city, who was the daughter of Major Fairlie, formerly clerk of the Supreme Court. After the death of her mother and the reverses which attended the fortune of her father, she for a short time appeared upon the stage. It was deemed a necessity and she submitted to it with grace. But it was said she often fainted away after the performance of a character, and was never happy while a professional person. Her sweetness of manner and strength of mind, added to a very lady-like appearance, won the heart of Mr. Robert Tyler, to whom she is very tenderly attached.

On her marriage she withdrew from the stage and devoted herself to the duties of private life. Called by unforeseen circumstances to become prominent in the leading circles of society, she has shown all the power of her native strength of mind, and without being dazzled by the elevation of her position, has preserved the beauty of her early character.

She has sound judgment, great discretion, a keen perception of the true and the false, and is a warm friend to those entitled to her confidence and esteem. She has made no enemies; and without being affected by false flattery is alive to the good opinion of her friends. She understands human nature perfectly and is not easily deceived by mere professions.

She is indeed a lovely woman, and is not in the least insensible to the kind of reception given to her husband's father by the people of her native city.

May she long enjoy the health and happiness which a protecting Providence has awarded her.

Priscilla's diary and her letters give a fairly well connected story of her White House years, but, strangely enough, there is nothing in any of the personal records about the tragedy on the

Princeton, a disaster which changed the course of many lives. At eleven on a bright morning, February 22, 1844, the President, Mrs. Robert Tyler, her sister, Louisa Cooper, John Tyler, Jr., Dolly Madison, David Gardiner and his queenly daughter, Julia, together with a number of other distinguished guests, assembled on board a steamer which was to carry them to Alexandria, where the *Princeton* awaited them.

As they approached, the guns thundered a welcome, and the band struck up a tune. On the flag-bedecked boat an elaborate luncheon was served on the lower deck. The President seemed especially interested in conversation with Julia Gardiner. When the men went upstairs after the meal to examine the cannon in the bow, he remained below. If he had accompanied the other gentlemen, he might have lost his life in the explosion which took place, when, at Secretary Gilmer's request, the Captain gave orders to fire a round of ammunition. The big gun burst, killing Gilmer, as well as Gardiner, Upshur, Commodore Kennon, a number of sailors, and the President's bodyservant.[41]

Julia Gardiner, grief-stricken at the death of her father, turned to John Tyler for comfort. The fact that he was fifty-four and she twenty-four did not deter them from falling in love. Priscilla fostered the affair, not only because she loved the President and wanted his happiness, but because the marriage offered an opportunity for her to leave her responsibilities in good hands. For some time she had felt that a government job, no matter how good, was not her conception of a career for Robert and that her own dizzy honors were a poor substitute for family life under normal conditions. She had begged Robert to delay no longer his intention to start the practice of law. When it became obvious that the President would marry Julia Gardiner within the year, Robert agreed that since Priscilla was willing to face poverty and hard work, to give up the comfort of the White House, he was also. Fortunately Mrs. Semple, President Tyler's daughter, was free to take charge for the interval between the departure of the Robert Tylers in March and their father's marriage in June.

Priscilla left the President reluctantly. She wrote Julia Gardiner that in the five years she had lived with him he had never opened his lips but to speak words of love to her and her children, that every action of his life towards her had been dictated by affection and kindness.[42]

On this harmonious note ended a period of intimate association that had been apparently without discord. The Robert Tylers went to Philadelphia, and began to lead lives of their own, more or less independent of the success or failure of John Tyler's political fortunes, but they were always bound to him by strong ties of respect and affection.

7

LEAN TIMES FOR THE TYLERS

1844-1850

PRISCILLA'S COURAGE when she first stepped upon the stage to play Virginia to her father's Virginius was loudly applauded; her poise as she stood, young and apparently unafraid, by President Tyler's side, welcoming the guests of the nation to the White House, excited admiration; but the fortitude she displayed in the tragic years 1844 to 1850 had no admiring audience. No flattery sustained it; no public approval gave it sanction—only the love she bore her husband and children made her life bearable.

Once before, when she gladly relinquished stardom for marriage, she had made with good grace the transition from public to private life; but in urging her husband to leave his pleasant and profitable position in the Land Office for the practice of law in Philadelphia, she was risking more than her own happiness; involved in the change was the welfare of Robert Tyler, their daughters, Mary Fairlie and Letty, and an unborn child. It was, therefore, with a heavy heart and many misgivings she said good-by to her father-in-law, Dolly Madison, the Websters, and her other Washington friends.

The Secretary of State gave her as a parting gift two dozen Bohemian champagne glasses—twelve, ruby red; twelve, white crystal.[1] It seemed a present she would not be likely to use in the simple life she and Robert planned; but at her suggestion, the President promised to send several bottles of champagne so that they might drink his health and that of his bride on the Presidential wedding day, now only three months off. In parting, Priscilla begged him not to let Julia be so fascinating after they were married that he and everyone else would forget the former mistress of the White House; however, she wanted him and the world to know she was quite contented with the life she and her husband had chosen for themselves. In her letters to Washington after she was settled in their Philadelphia lodgings, she said nothing about how much they all missed the comforts of the Mansion and its spacious grounds, or how much it taxed her ingenuity to find amusement for the children in their cramped quarters, while Robert studied all day and half the night in a zealous attempt to get off his bar examinations. His diligence made her increasingly confident that it would not be long before he was admitted to practice. When he had become attorney for a number of affluent clients, then she promised herself the bliss of looking at the children and knowing they had a chance to live properly and be provided for.[2]

By the first of June it seemed that realization of this dream grew nearer day by day; however, a flurry of political excitement upset everything. John Tyler could hardly have had illusions about there being any possibility of his retaining his high office for a second term; but he let himself be nominated in 1844 as the choice of a newly organized group, made up of those who were dissatisfied with the Whig and the Democratic parties. He wished above all things to put through the legislation necessary to insure the annexation of Texas—if not before his term expired, then in the next administration. Van Buren, the proposed Whig candidate, opposed the Texas plan. The President was determined at whatever cost to himself, to swing the election to the Democratic nominee, Polk, by stepping out in his favor in return for a pledge concerning annexation. This intention was a secret carefully guarded; in the meantime the Tyler faction behaved as if they intended to fight to win. Conventions were held in Baltimore, Philadelphia, and New York, and so many voters flocked to the banner of "the Democratic Republicans," that the Whigs were mildly alarmed and the "Polkites" became eager for a coalition.[8] There were plots and counter plots, and a great deal of political bargaining, much more fascinating to Robert Tyler than his books. Abandoning his resolution to put his career as a lawyer above all other considerations, he went back to Washington.

All of the letters that passed between Priscilla and her husband are filled with evidence of their devotion to each other. About most things they were completely in accord; but his desire to add new glories to the name of Tyler and his comparative indifference to earning a living for her and his children were for many years to give his wife real concern. This was the third occasion since their marriage on which he had sacrificed his own prospects to those of his father—a course of action he considered family loyalty, but of which Priscilla did not approve. In a letter to him, written June 4, 1844, she expressed eloquently her objection to his yielding once again to "the seduction of politics."

At last, my dear husband, I have received a letter from you, after a whole week's passing without a single line. My mind was exceedingly relieved at finding you were not sick, which I had taken it into my head was the case from your long silence.

I am sorry to see you still so sanguine as to Father's election. The very selection of Polk and Dallas was intended to work against Father as much as anyone else. Polk they thought the only man General Jackson would prefer to the President, and Dallas they chose to withdraw the support of Wilkins, Walker, etc. Is not Mr. Calhoun behaving strangely—or rather his friend? They have pledged the support of South Carolina for Polk, and Mr. Cohen of Georgia (a Calhoun man) has promised Georgia. Altogether I have never felt so vexed and pained at the absolute injustice done to Father; it has made me really sick and miserable.

Of course the Polkites want a union ticket. . . . They cannot succeed without Father's assistance. With that, I have no doubt the Democratic party will be successful, as they have stolen the Texas question, besides using the veto issue and all of Father's ammunition. I should consent to the union ticket if I were in Father's place, but I should bargain for the protection of my friends if I did. But the next best thing is to withdraw and be disinterested and help the democracie[sic] and get you a good foreign mission.

What are your future plans for the future when you return here? Are you opening your office or will this political excitement still continue? The first wish of my heart, my dearest husband, is that you may return and decisively go into the practice of the law, giving up everything else. You say that Father wishes me to come to Washington to be confined. If you intend being in Philadelphia, of course I must be here, for I cannot with any happiness be longer separated from you. If you cannot yet settle down to law, I certainly will comply with Father's wishes, for it is madness for us to live at the expense we do here without any object—and great injustice to your father. But I still cling to the hope, dearest, that you will return here with a full determination to go into your office and suffer no interruption in your determination of acquiring a name and subsistence. To leave Philadelphia, uncomfortable as it is, after having moved, bag and baggage, taken an office, etc., without having done anything would exceedingly mortify me, and be like the King of France, who "with twenty thousand men marched up a hill, and then marched down again!"

My dear husband, you must return to Philadelphia, give up the life of political care and excitement in which you live, find your dearest happiness in your wife and children, whose warmest affections are yours, and have the pleasure of moulding your own fortunes. God bless you, my beloved husband. Come back soon, determined "to do or die" at the law, and give happiness to your own devoted wife.[4]

John Tyler saw the letter, for he wrote on the margin a note: "The advice you give Robert is excellent. J. T." The President himself might with advantage have acted on her suggestion that he "bargain for the protection of his friends"; for Polk, once in power, was to forget after he was in office what he owed to the man who was partly responsible for his election, and to treat shamefully many whom Tyler had appointed. Fortunately the legislation affecting Texas was not left in his hands but was rushed through in time to bear Tyler's signature.[5] One of the few promises the victorious candidate kept, of many made in secret caucuses, was the appointment of Tom Cooper to a well paid, easy position as inspector of customs in New York City—a sinecure the old actor eagerly accepted, being thoroughly weary of his exile in Frankford.[6]

Robert went back to his interrupted studies once more, and Priscilla awaited the birth of her third child in the unrelenting heat of the city in mid-summer. Mary Fairlie and Letty began to look pale and lose their appetites; so their mother sent them to Fire Island with a kind and competent friend, partly to enjoy the cool sea breezes and partly to have them out of the way when the expected baby arrived in July.[7]

In the vacuum caused by their absence, she and Robert settled down in earnest to plain living. When John Tyler married Julia Gardiner, June 28, they did not even consider the extravagance of attending the festivities. Julia sent the top layer of the wedding cake for them to sample; but there were so many requests for bits of it to dream on that Priscilla asked the President to have Wilkins, the cook, bake a cake especially for her to distribute to his admirers among her Philadelphia acquaintances.[8]

The Robert Tylers had almost immediately collected about them a pleasant circle of friends. They were a delightful couple and were from the first well known and well liked in their new home. The affection of the Meyers, the Riches, the Mierckens, and the Gratzes for the Cooper girls had not lapsed with the passing of years; and Robert came to know intimately many of the professional men with whom he was associated. They had friends to rejoice with them when their first son, John Tyler IV—"a child too beautiful to live"—was born in July, 1844.

It had been a century since the law of primogeniture had been operative in Virginia, but there still lingered among old families like the Tylers a tradition that the acquisition of a male heir called for special jubilation. As yet Robert had nothing to bequeath his boy except his father's and grandfather's honorable name, but he and Priscilla felt a great satisfaction at having done their part toward carrying on the Tyler dynasty. Uncomfortably crowded in poor lodgings and short of cash, they were; but when the little girls came home, sturdy and brown, and Priscilla was able once again to perform her household tasks, the family felt they had all they needed for future happiness.

Tragedy struck unexpectedly in February of the next year (1845). Little Mary Fairlie Tyler was taken ill with a wasting disease, diagnosed as "summer complaint" and considered incurable. The child grew steadily weaker in spite of the frantic efforts of her parents. They took her to Fire Island and to Williamsburg in hopes that a change of air would be beneficial, but after four months of illness she died.[9] In all Priscilla's anxiety and heartbreak Robert never left her; his tenderness and strength sustained her. When the little girl had been laid to rest in the cemetery at New Kent by the side of her Grandmother Tyler, the bereaved parents faced the future despairingly. Not only were they burdened by sorrow, but they found themselves deep in debt. It was in a desperate effort "to starve themselves down to their income" that they went to live in Bristol, in a tiny house called Willow Cottage.[10] It rented for sixty dollars a year; for ten dollars more annually Robert bought a ticket on the steamer that allowed him to come twice a week to see his wife and children. Priscilla, too much alone, staggered desolately from one domestic crisis to the next; while Robert battled for a living in the city and took the uncomfortable trip back and forth whenever he could.

In spite of obstacles, he made progress in his profession. Julia Tyler wrote Mrs. Gardiner, her mother, on July 22, 1845, that he was "going on slowly but surely." She added, "Were it not for his pride, he would get along faster and better; but he can neither beg nor do a mean thing. The other night he made a temperance speech for the orphans and drew in money, hundreds and hundreds, for them."[11]

Robert's consideration for Priscilla's wishes kept him from entering actively into politics; compromising between inclination and duty, he arrived at a judicious balance: by hard work at the office he supported his family; at the same time an active interest in civic affairs won for him recognition as a public figure. In 1844, the previous year, he had been elected President of the Irish Repeal Association, an office that offered a strategic foothold for a man interested in building up influence with all types of people

For all his high idealism, he was shrewd enough as a politician to realize that the Irish polled a tremendous vote in Pennsylvania.

Priscilla, pinching pennies and struggling with crying babies, understood what he was doing and did not protest, when by a speech such as Julia mentioned he made hundreds of dollars for others. It is quite clear, however, that Mrs. John Tyler thought such eloquence could be more profitably employed in court. Very naturally she felt that no matter what the Ex-President had owed his son in the past, the time had come for Robert to stop calling on his father. He should fill his own empty pockets in preference to the coffers of a charitable institution. Julia had a right to an opinion, for she was already embarking on a career of motherhood, which knew no pause until she had borne the aging John Tyler seven children.

It is remarkable that except for an occasional intimation on Julia Tyler's part that her step-son was impractical and that Mrs. Robert Tyler held her head too high,[12] there is no hint of discord in all the intimate correspondence between the members of the families. Priscilla apparently loved Robert's people, admired them without reservation, and felt sure of their love for her.

She did not, however, impose upon their affection when it was within her power to spare them. So long as she lived on or with them, she had shown a proper delicacy about inviting her family to be with her. However, it gave her, once settled in Willow Cottage, great satisfaction to have Cooper come each week end from New York, where he was now employed in the Customs Office. He was at this time a portly old gentleman with a ruddy face and silvery hair—quite an impressive figure when, dressed all in white, he came that summer to see his daughter.[13]

At the cottage he always caused a great deal of confusion. He and Robert frequently indulged in heated arguments about politics, and every meal became an adventure. Cooper was still as discriminating about good food and as easily outraged by bad as on the day long ago when he suddenly left Ludlow, a theatrical friend who was dining with him in a New Orleans restaurant, because his guest put mustard on a choice mutton chop.

"Mutton chops and mustard!" he is reported to have exclaimed. "Great Heavens! I have heard of Yankee pork and molasses, but mustard and mutton! I can't stand that, nor will I sit at the table and countenance such barbarity!"[14]

His standards were high for the culinary arts. If he brought home from the city market oysters, game, or fresh salmon, he would follow Priscilla into the kitchen and supervise her supervision of the maid.

"Not that butter!" the powerful voice would thunder in portentous tone. "Any damn butter is good enough to eat but only the best to cook with."[15]

Later at the table there would be considerable domestic tension till he had tasted and approved each dish. Then his enjoyment of the meal would be pleasant to see. Priscilla liked to cater to his appetite. His amiable eccentricities amused her; and though his overpowering presence filled the small house, literally and figuratively, it crowded out her obsession with her sorrow over the loss of her idolized first-born. His company was probably more wholesome for her at this time than that of her sisters would have been. They wrote Priscilla letters filled with overflowing sympathy and offered to come if they were needed, but Priscilla declined their help, knowing that Mary Grace, Olivia and Julia could not be spared by their own households and that Virginia and Louise would not relish a life of exile in Bristol.

Neither her father's presence, the love of those closest to her, nor the passage of time assuaged Priscilla's bitter grief at losing Mary Fairlie. When about a year later, John Tyler, her son, died, she was dazed by the second blow, bereft of all desire to live. Little John's death was most sudden. When she put him in his carriage so that his nurse might take him for an airing, he was rosy and apparently quite well; when he returned an hour later, he was dying.[16]

There are no letters dealing with the months between July, 1845, when this tragedy occurred, and May, 1846, when Grace was born. Priscilla was in a dangerous mental and physical condition after her confinement, following, as it did, so closely upon the loss of her two children. Robert borrowed money and took her to Alabama.

Mary Grace's home, Longwood, was fairly large and its hospitality elastic. When Mr. and Mrs. Robert Tyler, Susan Poor, the old nurse, and the two children arrived, Olivia and her husband, Alfred McDonald, were living there; Cooper and Louisa were on a visit. No one was put out by the presence of five additional guests. The house servants, Sukey, Selma, Jacob, and the grey-haired Rose, efficiently supervised by Mary Grace, looked after things and saw that the guests were comfortable. After the austerities of Willow Cottage, plantation life seemed luxurious. Robert wished he could give up the struggle in Philadelphia; he talked idly of going to Texas, where land was rich, and establishing himself there.[17] But as soon as he saw Priscilla safely settled, he went back dutifully to the practice he dared not neglect.

During the first months Priscilla was prostrated. Her letters to Robert were full of tears; she kept to her room and was afflicted by all manner of distressing nervous symptoms.[18] After a time, thanks to the healing presence of her elder sister, she improved. She began gradually to take an interest in the life of the community. The neighboring gentry—the Scotts, the Armisteads, the Lucases, the Taylors—called and were called upon, invited them to dine and were dined in return. Mt. Meigs was, as Priscilla found, not at all dull but a "brisk little place." Something was always happening. Pelot, the school master, did what he could to pound sense into the heads of his patrons' sons. Likewise he tried to battle against the cultural inertia of the grown-up Charleses, Raouls, Campbells, Mitchells, Pinkstons, Murdocks, and the rest.

He was the moving spirit in a remarkable organization, the heart of the social life of the community. It was known as the Primary Society of Promoters and stated its aims modestly as "The modification and improvement of human society and the practice of charity." Its minutes, still in possession of Tom Taylor's heirs at Chantilly, show that there were a constitution, by-laws, a secret sign, secret motto, and the like. The number of elected officers—eleven in all—included a surveyor, an adjutant, an admonitor, a charger, a secretary, a conductor, a tester, a reflector, a marker, a Merry Andrew, and a terpsichorean. Since the society was limited to thirty-five, it must have been difficult to be a member without portfolio. Louisa and Thomas Cooper were regularly enrolled, as were, of course, Frederic and Mary Grace. The Tylers were made honorary members. The Raouls were leaders in getting up the plays and bazaars by which the society made money for its charities. Cooper when he came on a visit was invaluable as a coach when something of a dramatic nature was attempted.[19]

Priscilla was immensely diverted by the fierce enmities that sprang up in the group and the jealousies that threatened to disrupt those who had organized to reform the world and practice charity. All the unattached males—and some of those loosely attached—fell a little in love with the frail and beautiful "Lady in White,"[20] who entered eagerly into all their plans and discussions. The admiration and kindness her presence excited in Mary's and Frederic's friends and relatives cheered her spirits; rest and the good food—the hams, chickens, and turkeys, the custard and sponge cake—that came regularly upon Mary Grace's table helped her to regain her health. When Robert came for her the following spring she was well enough to return to Bristol by a leisurely route, stopping in Charleston with the Pinckneys but unfortunately not being able to stay quite long enough to see her old friends, Mr. and Mrs. Daniel Webster, who were expected shortly.

On their way home the Tylers spent a week in Washington, where Robert had business. Priscilla sounded almost like herself in describing this visit.

> Our visit in Washington was a very pleasant one. We were completely surrounded by our old friends. Every servant that had lived with us came to see us: Old Ben, the cook, Aunt Millie, Smith, John Wilkins, and all the gardeners. I had a bouquet every day from the President's garden.

Mrs. Adams, Mrs. Madison—everyone that is anyone—came to see us, and seemed so full of kindness and feeling that I was quite over-powered. I never realized before that the Washington people liked me for myself. And so many compliments. The White House had never been what it was when I was there. . . .[21]

After they reached Bristol, apprehension about the children and heavy domestic responsibilities, she wrote Mary Grace, made her wish, just at first, to be back at Longwood.

And such a time as I have had since I have been here. Mrs. Poor left me at her door. I have not *smelt* her since [one week]. Grace misses her terribly. Tish is as meddlesome as possible—and climax of horrors! Papa arrived here just one hour after we did, and only left this morning. I have the most tremendous cold I have ever had in my life. Cough all night and dreadful sleepiness all day from laudanum I take to stop the cough. Jeanette is my only assistant, until the last three days I have got a little girl to hold the baby, to whom, of course, Grace has taken the most terrific hatred, and won't stay with her five minutes at a time. Now is this not a concatenation of trouble? Do you think you could survive it? I assure you Sukey, Jacob and Selina are mere *circumstances!*[22]

"You have no idea how desolate I feel. I feel so alone," she wailed, echoing the emotion and even the phraseology of the complaints she and Mary Grace made when as girls they were separated from each other. There was, however, nothing sickly about Priscilla's devotion to her elder sister; her year with Mary Grace had strengthened, not weakened, her. Within a week, although her thoughts still dwelt lovingly on the pleasant time at Longwood, she celebrated her return to normal enjoyment of life:

What a happy winter I did pass with you, to be sure. No visit ever produced so good an effect. I really feel like a changed being. And now I look forward to your coming here next summer, and intend postponing getting my new sofa covers, etc., for that occasion. Now, mind, nothing is to disappoint me. Give my love to Loo and dear Frederic and Liv and Mc.

I don't believe that that quotation is in Shakespeare at all. . . . I have looked in every play but two and can't find it.

Why don't you write again? After your last letter we are in a terrible state of curiosity. What will happen? What will the society do? What a delicate business for you all. How difficult to manage it. I really pity you. The society, I am afraid, will break up. How do Mrs. Lucas and Judkins bear it? Do write me every particular—all Tom said and did. Poor Harriott! How dreadful for her! and Mrs. Campbell—and what will William do?

How comes on the society? Has Cella been proposed yet? Poor little Cella! Let me still be his guardian and propose him. I will vacate for him. Tell Mr. Lucas he must send me the minutes sometime to keep me *au fait*. Oh, his paper has come! It is rich. I cannot think that "the Lady in White" is intended for me. My family cannot quite swallow "the gloriously beautiful creature." The "ardent youths," I suppose, were Cella and that old fellow that played the melodian. They were the only ones that spoke to me during the evening. Give my compliments to Mr. Lucas and tell him we received the paper, and are much obliged to him, though we think him rather complimentary.

I have been to Philadelphia once lately. Had ice cream on purpose to think of you. I took Tish to see Tom Thumb, and certainly he is the greatest curiosity I ever saw. Not so tall as Grace and perfectly proportioned; with little hands and feet like hers; weighing only fifteen pounds; dressed in a complete little man's suit; with a hat on his head; a very pretty face; and no sort of deformity at all. Full of fun and frolic. I would give anything if Tom and Theus could see him. He kissed Tish, much to her horror.

Pa left us yesterday after spending four days again with me. Came on Saturday about two, with salmon to cook for dinner. I with no cook. Papa was not well when he came—with a cough, which someone put in his head arose from the elongation of his palate and that it should be cut. He wanted to have it done as soon as he got here, but I persuaded him not. He has been very anxious that I should have Grace's and Tish's to be cut. He got perfectly well again, with a good appetite before he left, and went off abusing the man for a damn fool that wanted him to have his palate cut.[23]

Her good spirits reflect not only her improved health but recent release from economic strains. In 1847 Robert was appointed solicitor to the sheriff of Philadelphia. His assured income enabled him to pay his debts presently and to move his family into more comfortable quarters.[24]

The letters that went back and forth between Bristol and Mt. Meigs from 1847 to 1849 are so filled with discussions of children's diseases and household emergencies—with all the things important to the two matrons and unimportant to anyone else—that they do not repay quotation or even summary. Only when Cooper was at Willow Cottage does anything occur more important than Grace's learning to talk or Letty's getting a well-deserved spanking.

Priscilla's eldest daughter was six and getting to be "a handful." She told her mother the Devil was in her, that she could hear him clearly telling her what to do.[25] And really it seemed that she had an instinct for naughtiness. On one occasion she made her grandfather swear. Usually Cooper softened his vocabulary for the children's ears. He had picked up from Shakespeare's plays and other dramatic literature a remarkable selection of violent language, which though highly appropriate for the expression of his own displeasure, sounded shocking when Letty repeated to her mother what he had said.[26] Priscilla was more amused than dismayed.

Reckless about exposing himself to drafts and over-exertion, Cooper was almost as much a care as the children. The infirmities of age he ignored; but he was always involved with some health fad. He brought home a galvanator with which he proposed to shock himself into youthful vigor. And though Priscilla feared the Devil would suggest to Letty the advisability of electrocuting Grace, she made no protest. The summer of '48 when Priscilla's second son, Thomas Cooper Tyler, was born, Cooper conceived the idea that flies were dangerous and wanted to keep all the doors and windows closed to protect the baby. He disliked Robert's smoking a pipe and was seized with paroxysms of coughing whenever he saw even an unlighted one.[27]

Retired from his post in the New York Customs in 1846, he was thereafter free to spend his summers in Bristol, his winters in Alabama, where the mild climate made his catching cold less to be feared. Plantation life reminded him of the happy times long ago in Carolina, when he had liked to hunt and fish with Huger. In Mt. Meigs he shot partridges with his crony, Tom Taylor. He had always been a better marksman with a pistol than with a gun, but, taking his age into consideration, he acquitted himself well in the field. He was sought after as a dinner guest by the Raouls' friends among the planters, for he could hold his own in any company as a pleasant companion.

He was ailing when he came North in the spring of 1849. Julia Campbell hurried down from New York to help Priscilla care for him. The old man was very good and patient under the ministrations of his two daughters; but he did not improve.

Countless times upon the stage he had spoken effectively the dramatic last words of a hero. Macbeth's, Othello's, Lear's or Hamlet's farewells to the world, as he delivered the eloquent lines, had moved his audience to tears; but he died very quietly, without histrionics of any sort. The parish register of the Episcopal Church in Bristol records his death as taking place April 20, 1849. Immediately below, in July of that same year, there occurs another tragic entry: "The burial of Robert Tyler's child." Thomas Cooper Tyler, his grandson, had lived only two years—a brief life indeed compared to the three score and thirteen years of the famous grandfather whose name he bore. Both the child and the old man were buried beside Mary Fairlie Cooper under the trees in St. James's churchyard.[28]

8

PROLOGUE TO DISASTER

1850-1860

THOSE WHO claim to find a delicate balance between the good and evil fortune that comes to men, might discern in the years 1850 to 1860 the principle of compensation at work in the lives of the Robert Tylers. Following seven years of tragedy, climaxed by the death of Priscilla's father and her baby son, there came ten years of happiness and prosperity.

Born to them on October 15, 1849, was another child, a little daughter, who was given her mother's name but was called "Tousie" by members of the family.[1] Shortly after her birth they moved to Philadelphia. Robert had endured long enough the discomfort of lodgings in the city; there was no reason why he should not now have his family with him, for his solicitorship paid well and he had acquired a good private practice.

Distressed as Priscilla doubtless was at leaving Bristol, she could not have failed to be delighted with the new home at 186 Rowlandson's Row, for it had the conveniences which were considered luxuries in 1850—a bathroom upstairs, where water was piped into a long tin tub, and gas all over the house. Greatly admired by callers were two beautiful bronze chandeliers, with four globes each, in the adjoining parlors. When all the lights were on at once it was as bright as day. She had gathered together as many of her mother's old things as could be reclaimed. An old-fashioned sofa, a pier glass, and several handsome chairs gave the room dignity. The bust of Napoleon, given to her father by Joseph Bonaparte, had the place of honor on the mantel in the front drawing room.[2] This comfort and elegance must have afforded great satisfaction to both Mr. and Mrs. Robert Tyler as tangible evidence of his enterprise and her taste. By seven years of application they had accomplished the minor miracle of paying off all their debts and achieving a moderate degree of economic security. When John Tyler, Sr., and his family came for a visit, Julia was surprised at how well they lived and at how many of "the best people" came to call.[3] While his father was there, Robert proudly demonstrated his solvency by taking him to the haberdasher's and buying him a hat and a suit of clothes. Priscilla did not have the heart to reprove her husband's extravagance,[4] for she doubtless saw in the generous act a personal declaration of independence. Except for Robert's unsatisfied political ambitions, he and Priscilla would now have been at peace with the world if their little sons had lived to carry on the name. Philoprogenitiveness seems to have been for several generations a Tyler trait. Robert's grandfather, Judge Tyler, had three boys and five girls of his own and reared in his home twenty-one other children for whom he was guardian. He used to sit under the trees at Greenways, his estate near Williamsburg, and play tunes for them on his violin and tell them stories.[5] Robert's own father had fourteen children by his two wives. Although everyone was disappointed when on January 5, 1852, Priscilla bore a fourth daughter instead of the boy they all wanted, no one grumbled about there being another mouth to feed. The healthy, good-natured baby was named Elizabeth and straightway became a great favorite with her sisters, Letitia, Grace, and Tousie.

The following summer Priscilla had further cause to rejoice when Mary Grace wrote that she planned to come with Tom and Theus, her two children, for a long visit. Frederic Raoul sent his family North to escape the danger of yellow fever, which was that year epidemic in and around Montgomery. When the travellers arrived, there was so much to say the sisters thought they never would be done talking. For days Mary Grace could not find time to write to "poor, dear, deserted Fred," who was much on her mind and heart. He had been obliged to remain at Longwood to get in the crop; but he had promised to come as soon as frost fell, to accompany his wife on the journey home. Otherwise, she would not have left him, even though his sister, Mrs. Tom Taylor, would see that the servants looked after his needs.[6]

As soon as Priscilla and Mary Grace had sufficiently admired each other's children and had caught up on family news, they went shopping. Fred had given his wife, his son and his daughter plenty of money to spend, for these were the days when the Southern planters had cash, and Cotton was King. The aunts and cousins had entrusted Mary Grace with additional small sums to be spent for them on such items as cutlery for Olivia McDonald or harp strings for Mrs. Charles. Later she attended to these commissions with her customary efficiency, but her first purchase was a hat for herself and one for Theus, for which she paid three dollars apiece.[7] Priscilla and Robert told her that if Fred could see her in the becoming lilac bonnet, faced with white, with the ribbons tied under her chin, he would fall in love with her all over again.

The stores fascinated the Raoul children. Theus "spent as she went," and was soon the proud possessor of a tea set, a doll, and a music box. Tom pondered his needs, and hoarded his money, greatly to the admiration of his mother, who tried to emulate his example. She wanted every cent to count, and lived in a delicious agony of desiring everything she saw and virtuously restraining herself from indulging her lavish impulses.

Priscilla was amused at the range and intensity of Mary Grace's desires. She wanted a gadget manufactured by the Singer Sewing Machine Company, on sale for $125, but was skeptical about it, and would not believe that the coats, pantaloons, and waistcoats hanging in the store were sewed by it until she saw some stitching done.[8] She longed for a sausage grinder, which could cut up a whole tub full of meat in no time. But of all the things she saw that took her eye, daguerreotypes at seventy-five cents apiece appealed to her most. She had one each of Priscilla, Mr. Tyler, and all the children; of herself and her friend, Estelle Meyers—seventeen in all. She denied herself a "Talbotype" that she yearned to have made of Fred, because it cost too much. Of course the daguerreotype she had of him was good, but it reversed the image; whereas the Talbotype would have shown him as he was, "with his bumps on the right side."[9]

Priscilla found her sister the dearest guest in the world—eager and interested in everything. She was an enthusiastic visitor at an institution for the blind, a home for the deaf, a horticultural exhibit, a jewelry factory, and a foundry; and had a great deal to say about them all, except the foundry, which she did not understand. She went to church twice on Sunday and really listened to the sermons. She heard Sontag sing and enjoyed anything they happened to see at the theatre.

She was much easier to amuse than her twelve-year-old son and nine-year-old daughter. Everyone was disgusted by the assumed sophistication of Tom and Theus. It was the first time they had ever been off the plantation, but they had no idea of showing any admiration for anything. They behaved "like Indians," never changing their expressions when they saw the Delaware River for the first time or went to the theatre. They did not want their Yankee cousins to know they were impressed, and suggested by their indifference that rivers in Pennsylvania were nothing to rivers in Alabama, and that Mr. Pelot's singers in Mt. Meigs were infinitely superior to the Virginia Serenaders, performing that week at the local playhouse.[10]

Priscilla was glad when this unnatural hauteur wore off and they played happily with their little cousins. Except when Tom ran after fire engines, which he found the most exciting thing in the city, the children were safe with the servants, and she and Mary Grace were free to see old friends—the Baches, the Phillipses, the Mierckens, and especially Ann and Estelle Meyers, Grace and Juliana Riche. Nearly every night they went calling or entertained visitors. If they stayed at home, Mary Grace played on the piano and everyone danced. They ate ice cream—"lovely pyramids of it"—at fifty cents a quart till Tom looked "stuffed into his clothes," and Robert Tyler called Mary Grace "Butterball."[11]

As a sad result of such indulgence, Tom had to have a new outfit. His mother found a tailor who would make him a very stylish suit for $3.75, which she thought a trifle high but perhaps a wise investment.[12] She let out the seams in her own dresses and bought a new black silk which she hoped would give a "subdued effect to the superabundance" of her figure. It was easier to make such adjustments than to resist Priscilla's special dishes: minced veal, marrow bones, sweetbreads, oysters and wonderful breads of all kinds.

Mr. Tyler hired an omnibus and took them on several expeditions. When they went to Fairmont on the banks of the Schuylkill River, Tom and Grace got lost—on purpose, the children said, for they thought Tom in love with his little cousin and teased him unmercifully.[13]

Several times they spent the day in Bristol, going and coming on the steamer. Priscilla and Mary Grace wrote to the widely scattered members of the Cooper family about the neglected graves in the cemetery, and made plans to erect headstones inscribed with the names of their mother and father and little brothers. They found that their former home on Radcliffe Street had changed very little, and their old friends not at all, in so far as affection for them was concerned. The sisters visited everyone, even the old servant, Mrs. Poor, and met everywhere with kindness.

It seemed so right to have Mary Grace with her that Priscilla kept urging her to delay her trip to Newark and New York; but when September came and it began to grow cool, it was inevitable that she must go—first to visit Virginia Cooper, now Mrs. Thorburn, and then to spend a few days with Julia Fairlie Ogden and her family.

She found Ginny greatly improved by prosperity, living in a beautiful place on the Passaic River, just opposite Newark. She had been the ugly duckling among the pretty Cooper girls, and everyone had been surprised when, after a brief debut in New York, she had made what seemed at the time an exceedingly advantageous match. The kind, already bald, middle-aged man she married was the son of Grant Thorburn, so outstanding an example of the "rags to riches" tradition in America that an English woman had written a book about him, called *Laurie Todd.* He himself wrote *Forty Years Residence in America* to tell the story of his success. As an emigrant from Scotland, he had landed in New York with sixpence in his pocket, set up as a florist and prospered so amazingly that it was not long before he had quite an establishment in Newark—vast greenhouses, filled with exotic blooms among which caged birds sang. Visiting celebrities always made a pilgrimage to see this proof of the fact that in America anything is possible to a man who is thrifty.[14]

Ginny's husband was not so good a business man as his father; but at the time of Mary Grace's visit the Thorburns were living in luxury. The house was filled with pictures and statues and imported china, possessions more impressive than Ginny's little husband. He was kindness itself to his wife's sister and the children, and Mary Grace approved of him thoroughly.[15]

Louisa Cooper was there visiting, and had the household stirred up about spiritualism, her latest fad. Nothing would do but that they must go out and buy a table suitable for the purpose of table-rapping. Ginny was an obliging hostess; she bought the table and they spent a diverting evening in the spirit world. Mary Grace immediately began to plan to astonish Mt. Meigs social circles upon her return by giving a seance. She wrote to Fred to have everything in readiness.[16]

It was too bad Priscilla could not have gone with them when the three sisters and the children went for a spree to New York on Saturday, October 4, 1852. They made a day of it! First they saw Trinity Church, a sight well worth their pains. Next they got in an omnibus and drove through the city to 42nd Street, "the new part of town." For lunch at a good restaurant they had oysters, ham, hot muffins, butter, coffee and ice cream, which excellent meal cost twenty cents apiece. There was an orgy of shopping at Stewart's—a store four stories high, employing 300 clerks. At Barnum's Museum they saw not only curiosities but a play beautifully performed, one with so high a moral tone that Mary Grace was glad she had the children with her. All this was delightful but exhausting, and they were glad to get back to Newark that evening and find Mr. Thorburn waiting at the station with Mary Grace's shawl over his arm.[17]

She spent a day or two in Ravenswood with her aunt, Julia Fairlie Ogden, in her new home, a square house with a cupola, with lovely gardens and a cherry orchard that sloped down to the East River.[18] She could not have come more opportunely, for the Ogdens were rejoicing at the imminent settlement in their favor of a long-drawn-out lawsuit for $150,000 against the estate of John Jacob Astor. Everyone was in a good humor; the children behaved well and were properly admired.[19]

It was unfortunate that Mary Grace's visit came at a time when her sister, Julia Cooper Campbell, was not in New York. She had been for several years in South America with her husband. There Allan Campbell was engineer in charge of the first railroad built on that continent—a stretch of road from Calao to Lima. It always surprised the sisters that Julia, who had been as a girl a little lazy, should lead such a strenuous life. Lately she had written of riding with Allan mule-back across the Andes, carrying her small son before her on the saddle. Apparently she found the hazardous journey not too inconvenient, for as long as she was with her husband she felt safe.[20]

Before Mary Grace's return to Philadelphia there was a feeling of fall in the air; one morning she saw frost, so she knew that it would be safe to go home to Alabama. She came back to Priscilla's and in a bustle of shopping and packing spent a few confused days; but the visit was over. Louisa went South with her, since Fred had not been able to come. They chose the route down the Chesapeake to Wilmington and then inland.[21]

Just after her departure Robert became Prothonotary of the Supreme Court of Pennsylvania. His acceptance was yet another victory of Priscilla's prudence over his ambition. During Mary Grace's visit she had added her voice to her sister's in an effort to persuade him to take this excellent position, which paid well and would allow him to continue in private practice. They suspected that Robert's indecision was due to his hope of a lucrative appointment if Pierce were elected, and they did not want him to give up security for what Mary Grace called with mild scorn, "making a flourish in the world."

During the campaign of '52 he had been hand in glove with the Democratic nominee, and felt reasonably sure of a reward for his activities on the stump and in the press. He had stressed to the Irish voters, who trusted him, Pierce's liberal attitude towards those of Roman Catholic faith, and had won many votes for his candidate.

After the election Robert called on the victorious Franklin Pierce in the White House and wrote Priscilla about his visit there:

> I arrived here on Monday night. . . . The next day (yesterday) the President invited me to dinner; dined at five with the family and the Secretary of War. Mrs. Pierce was very gracious. In the evening the President asked me if I would not walk with him to see the new library and Capitol buildings and we went off arm and arm for two hours. The people started their eyes, but we walked on, conversing as wisely as if we had been the best (oldest) friends in the world. He is certainly a very pleasant gentleman and a man of great skill and courage. Today I met Mr. and Mrs. Semple and Ada Semple, Gen. S's daughter, a very pretty girl. I dine with Cushing and Dobbin at 5 o'clock. Tomorrow morning we expect to make tracks. They to New York, and your "Old Hubbie" homeward.
>
> Mr. Buchanan has just got home and has had a long and private interview with me and imparted secrets he has entrusted *to no other*. Did you ever see the like?[22]

Robert Tyler was addicted to politics in much the same way a drunkard is addicted to strong drink. Priscilla trembled for the future of the children whenever he was subjected to temptation. Fortunately his exciting hopes for high office, engendered by the walk arm-in-arm with the President, never materialized.

Robert accepted the position as Prothonotary, and although he did not give his exclusive attention to his own affairs, he did not put his passion for public life before his duty to his family. The Tylers settled down to serene domesticity for the next two years. Again in hopes of having a son to carry on the Tyler name, Priscilla bore a child—a fifth daughter, born on December 5, 1854. The family rapidly adjusted themselves to their disappointment and named the baby Julia Campbell for her aunt.

Eighteen fifty-six brought the excitement of another Presidential election, and letters went back and forth between Robert, his father and his brother in regard to the candidates. All the Tylers at first pinned their hopes on Henry A. Wise, Governor of Virginia,[23] the most ardent champion of the slaveholding South. However, when James Buchanan showed an interest in being nominated, Robert shifted his allegiance. Buchanan, Secretary of State under Polk, now Minister to England under Pierce—experienced in every field of political activity—was a reliable if not a brilliant prospect. This change of front was quite agreeable to Wise, who, like Warwick, preferred being king-maker to being king. They all remained friends, working closely and effectively together up to the opening of the convention in Cincinnati, May, 1856, at which the Democratic candidate would be chosen. At this meeting Robert enjoyed his first real political triumph. Carried away by excitement, he wrote to his father immediately afterwards:

> I met with a great deal of notice and consideration at the Convention, and your name was mentioned always with praise and admiration. My friends gave me a splendid banquet and a military escort. They have also ordered a full-length portrait to be taken for one of their halls. I made three or four speeches while I was in Cincinnati, but my banquet speech was the best. I was in the best temper possible and altogether pleased the company and myself—the latter a difficult thing to do. There was talk, at one time, about the possibility, under certain contingencies, of my name being suggested for Vice-President (Think of that!); but I laughed it off when mentioned to me as a good joke.

If I were a rich man, and the Union does not slide, I might be something yet.[24]

Although he did not neglect his duties as Prothonotary, as orator, journalist, and party lieutenant during the following months, Robert exceeded all his previous efforts at political campaigning. When the votes were counted, the Keystone State was overwhelmingly for Buchanan, and the successful candidate was quick to acknowledge his indebtedness to his friend. He did not, however, pay his debt promptly and generously. John Tyler, Jr., asked bitterly if "having squeezed the orange," Buchanan planned "to throw the rind away," and wrote eloquently to Wise about the ability of Robert Tyler, intimating that a position in the cabinet, "that tomb of politicians," would not be an adequate reward for the services his brother had rendered. Some more important position would under the circumstances be appropriate.[25]

Robert's comment was that there were only one or two appointments in which he was interested, for he regarded most of the positions in the cabinet as "mere clerkships."[26] Doubtless he realized that Cass had earned the position of Secretary of State—the only honor worth striving for. Since the cabinet was made up of conservatives, named as concessions and compromises rather than for ability, Robert Tyler may have realized that he did not wish to be a member of such a group. His intimacy with the newly elected President gave him the advantage of being able to decline an appointment he thought undesirable even before it was officially offered.

Priscilla was disappointed that Robert refused a commission in Switzerland. She wrote on November 21, 1856, to Julia Gardiner Tyler in regard to the matter:

. . . Mr. Buchanan told Mr. Tyler he might have anything he wanted and suggested the mission to Switzerland as instantly at his disposal. Now I should dearly love to go to Switzerland if Mr. Tyler's pecuniary affairs would only permit it. It is really a dreadful blow to me to be forced to decline it. It would take Mr. Tyler away from all the din and fury of party politics, from personal hostilities and from this vulgar, hurried turmoil of city life. It would educate our children well and cheaply. It would be a delightful change for myself, and altogether I think it would be very nice, quiet and dignified. But it is one of the day dreams I must give up & resign myself to "suckle fools and chronicle small beer!" Pretty much the alpha and omega of all women.

Of course I do not allow Mr. Tyler to suppose I have had any feeling of disappointment in the matter. He has enough to contend with, poor fellow. I feel as if I and the children were dreadful drags upon him. . . .[27]

The unbroken friendship between the Robert Tylers and Buchanan is eloquent testimony that Robert did not think the President acted with flagrant ingratitude. Even after differences in regard to the issues which brought on the Civil War divided them, there was great kindness in their feeling for each other. When Robert was fighting a losing battle with poverty during the evil days of Reconstruction, a check for a thousand dollars and a letter from the Ex-President came at a moment when he was desperately in need.[28]

Such astute observers of the political scene as John Tyler, Sr., and his sons were not unaware of the rapidily approaching crisis between the agrarian South and the industrial North. In the discussions, verbal and written, that went on ceaselessly between them they thrashed out every aspect of the Fugitive Slave Law in 1850, the Kansas-Nebraska Bill in 1854, and the legal technicalities of the long-drawn-out Dred Scott decision; but they were slow to realize the possibility of the country's resorting to arms as a means of settling what they considered a family quarrel. Having achieved a place in the sun, Robert saw the war clouds gathering but was reluctant to think them harbingers of more than a passing storm. He and Priscilla went about their lives as if bright days lay before them.

It had always been Priscilla's dream to return to Bristol and live not in a rented house but in a home of their own. They were fortunate in finding just what they wanted, an imposing residence at 610 Radcliffe Street, not far from the place where the Coopers had lived. It was on the river side of the street, too, with a garden even larger than the one in which she had played as a child. They were comfortably settled there before the birth of their last child, a son, born in December, 1857. His christening was quite an occasion. They waited until the baby's uncle, Allan Campbell, could stand as godfather for Robert Tyler, Jr. Mr. G. M. Dorrance, the Bristol historian, in his reminiscences says that little Robert was the first baby christened in the new Episcopal Church and that the water used in the ceremony was from the river Jordan in Palestine. After the service Mrs. Tyler gave a large dinner party.[29]

Mrs. Tyler entertained a great deal in these halcyon days and was entertained in turn. She often went with all the children to be the guest of her friend Mrs. Tyson, of Glenelg, Howard County, Maryland. It is pleasant to think of the two matrons, sitting sewing and chatting in the drawing room of this fine manor house. Two little colored girls, dressed alike in turkey-red cotton, with gold beads around their dusky throats, sat on either side of the ladies to thread their needles. The children played together in the garden; and young Harry, Mrs. Tyson's son, had his eye on Grace Tyler, the budding beauty, unmindful of the fact that Julia, the youngest of the Tyler girls, was one day to be his wife.[30]

The house on Radcliffe Street in Bristol was nothing like so grand as Glenelg, but Mrs. Tyson enjoyed coming there, as did Robert's and Priscilla's brothers, sisters and their children. Robert's political friends found a gracious welcome too, for Priscilla seemed at last to have made peace with her husband's ambition—the only rival she ever had in his affections.

Although prices were up and unemployment on the increase, it was an era of free spending. Long since, Mary Grace and Priscilla had sewing machines and had mastered their intricacies. The Raouls were planning to set up a carriage. Allan Campbell undertook the negotiations with such clear specifications in hand that nothing could have gone wrong. Presumably the instructions emanated from Frederic, but they have all the earmarks of Mary Grace's firmness and clarity of thought.[31] She evidently had in mind a vision of herself sitting proudly erect in an open carriage on olive-colored cushions, driving to church or to call upon the neighbors in Mt. Meigs, with her daughter, Theus, by her side, and Frederic and Tom in attendance. This was in 1859, so perhaps the worthy little lady had her dream come true—or perhaps it was in that carriage she sent Theus and Tom's young wife to Georgia when the Yankee raiders came in 1865.

Allan and Julia Campbell were prosperous too. They had moved from the Gramercy Park Hotel in New York to a home of their own on Lexington Avenue. Julia's letters are full of evidence of her own and her husband's generosity—a check for seventy-five dollars to the building fund of the Episcopal church contemplated at Mt. Meigs, the present of a blue dress with a slenderizing double skirt for Theus, and the like.[32]

Allan had been chief engineer of the New York and Harlem Railroad since 1856, and had recently been appointed its president. He was driving himself hard in an effort to improve the line—an undertaking in which he was associated with Commodore Vanderbilt. He was also controller and director in other money-making projects such as the Maryland Coal Company.[33] He and Julia planned to give their only child, Thomas Cooper Campbell, every possible advantage, and had sent him to a good school in Haverford. They were outgoing in their generosity and good to everyone in the family, especially Virginia Cooper Thorburn, who was having a lean time of it after her husband's death.[34] Louisa Cooper, Priscilla's youngest sister—now no longer a girl, was still unmarried, still pretty, and quick at repartee. She divided her time among her sisters, whose husbands enjoyed her visits as much as they did. Olivia Cooper McDonald seldom appears in the family letters. A story, still current in Mt. Meigs, declares that she educated her two sons herself—one in engineering and the other in law. Both were brilliant men who met with phenomenal success in their professions. There is nothing in the evidence to contradict this story and nothing to prove it true.

Jim Cooper, Priscilla's only brother, is in and out of the family records, always appearing as handsome and prosperous, with an air of breeding and distinction not unlike his father's. He was a successful construction engineer and came often to Alabama on business during the building of the Montgomery and Western Railroad, which was later called the Western Railway of Alabama.[35]

The year 1859 would be a propitious moment at which to end the story of the Coopers with the statement that they all lived happily ever after. Unfortunately, 1860 was to bring to them, as it did to many, change and misfortune.

Perhaps because they had more to lose, Priscilla and Robert suffered most. Robert was at the peak of his career in 1859 when he was made Chairman of the Pennsylvania State Central Democratic Committee. No horizon limited his future. He had laughed off the suggestion at the convention of 1856 that his name be brought up as a candidate for the Vice-Presidency, but several additional years had made a difference. He seems to have seriously entertained all manner of ambitions for the future; but the incident at Harper's Ferry in October, 1859, and the election of Lincoln a year later sealed his doom by ending all hope of a compromise between the warring factions in the country.

South Carolina, prompt to act, called a convention of the people immediately after the election and seceded December 20, 1860. By February 4, 1861, Georgia, Alabama, Mississippi, and Florida had joined their proud sister; and at a convention held in Montgomery, Alabama, had created The Confederate States of America. They adopted a constitution—a provisional one to be ratified later, chose Jefferson Davis as President and Alexander H. Stephens as Vice-President.

Letitia Tyler, Robert and Priscilla's eldest child, had a part to play in these fateful events. The Montgomery *Advertiser* of March 6, 1861, has in its columns this entry:

At a little after noon yesterday Congress adopted a flag for the Confederacy, which may be described thus: three bars, each in width one third of the depth of the flag; a blue field in the upper left-hand corner with seven stars in a circle. The secretary of the Congress was ordered to have a flag prepared and hoisted on the Capitol immediately and under the command of Commander Ingraham, and assisted by Lieut. Col. Sayre, late of the U. S. Marine Corps, the ensign of the federation was prepared and ready for hoisting a little before 4 o'clock P. M., when it was run up by Miss Tyler, a granddaughter of ex-President Tyler, in the presence of a considerable crowd. The Blues saluted the flag with seven guns and Mr. Canning's fine band from the theatre furnished excellent music for the occasion.

The Ex-President came out of his retirement at Sherwood to take an active part in the Peace Convention held in Washington in February, 1861. Disappointed when as the presiding officer of the group he failed in his negotiations, John Tyler recommended to the Virginia state convention immediate secession.

There was nothing equivocal in the stand taken by the Tylers, but neither of them expected the mob violence that began to stir against Robert. As the leading Democrat in Pennsylvania, he had said and he continued to say publicly in speeches and in the newspapers that he believed in states' rights and felt that under the Constitution the Southern planters were entitled to self-determination in the matter of slaves. These opinions, not surprising in a Virginian, smacked of heresy in his adopted state. He answered his critics with clearly reasoned statements of his political philosophy,[36] but expressed always complete loyalty to Pennsylvania.

I have not the least idea of leaving. . . . I have been a citizen of this state for seventeen years. I owe a debt of unceasing gratitude to this state for having given me my dear wife. My only son is a native of Bucks County, and my other children with one exception were born here. I have two children lying by the side of their maternal grandfather in the church yard at Bristol. I do not possess any pecuniary interest whatever outside this state . . . I may differ, perhaps, temporarily with a large majority in my political views, but I would sacrifice as much as any other citizen for the honor and dignity of the good old Commonwealth.[37]

By April 18, 1861, Ex-President John Tyler was alarmed at the threat of organized violence directed against his son and wrote to him:

I am much concerned at the notice of you given in the papers. What have you done to merit the threats of the Vigilance Committee? Write me without delay and let me know the true state of things.

Better leave than be under suspicion and surveillance. The rumor is that persons are not permitted to pass on South through Washington. Virginia is no longer a state of the old Union. She went out on the 16th.

In haste,

Yr. father
John Tyler[38]

His warning came too late. Something like the end of the world had already overtaken his son after the firing on Fort Sumter, April 12. At a meeting of citizens held on or before April 17 in Independence Square, a speaker mentioned Robert Tyler as a man who spoke always in defense of the South, and immediately there was wild clamor: "He ought to be lynched! He ought to be lynched!" One of his friends ran to his office to warn him. He hired a hack and was driven to Frankford, where he caught the train to Bristol. The crowd were hot on his heels, wishing to arrest him for treason. In Bristol he had been respected, but people who had once admired him now joined the mob which hunted him down as if he were a mad dog. Feeling ran so high that he was hanged in effigy by the light of bonfires built before his own home. He hid in the garret of a neighbor and next day went by steamer to New York. There Julia and Allan Campbell welcomed him kindly, although their political opinions were in opposition to his. From this temporary refuge he wrote to the mayor of Philadelphia, asking if he thought he would be molested if he returned, and was told that no one could guarantee him protection.[39]

We know from Priscilla's letters that she joined her husband in New York for a week, to confer with him about a course of action. Allan made arrangements for Robert to get to Richmond, and Julia and Louisa Cooper returned with Priscilla to Bristol to help her close the home there. One or two family portraits, the tea set George Washington had given Major Fairlie, the Gobelin tapestries Cooper had bought for his wife, the champagne glasses Webster had given Priscilla—a few prized possessions such as these were sent to Julia's for safe keeping, but everything else was to be sold by the sheriff to settle Robert's affairs, left in some confusion by his sudden departure.

In desperate haste not to be caught in the blockade, which everyone knew would soon be in effect, Priscilla made plans to leave. An appeal to an old friend, Major Craig Biddle, dated May 13, 1861, must have resulted in a pass through the lines.[40]

My dear Major Biddle:

May I ask a favor at your hands? I went to Philadelphia yesterday for the purpose of calling on General Patterson. Then it occurred to me you were one of his aides de camp and would take pleasure in doing for me that which it was embarrassing for me to do *for* myself *by* myself.

I am anxious to follow my husband to Virginia, and an opportunity offers for me to go next week with a clergyman from North Carolina. I have been told it would be necessary to procure a pass from General Patterson in case of any difficulty on the route.

I need not assure you that I carry no "comfort to the enemy" in any form. I am but a poor desolate woman with five children, seeking to be reunited to my husband, whose home has been broken up, whose peace has been invaded, and who has been forced to seek in another state the protection which he cannot find in this.

I could take the route via Alexandria, crossing over the long bridge at Washington City. The gentleman who accompanies me part of the way is Mr. Waln, a Northerner by birth and a strong Union man.

Will you remember me to your sisters most affectionately. The breaking up of my establishment here so suddenly and my every moment being so entirely occupied, I fear I shall find no time to see them before I leave.

Will you be so kind as to procure this pass for me from General Patterson, and oblige,

Yours very truly,
E. Priscilla Tyler

Leaving Bristol was not easy. She wrote to Mary from Richmond (May, 1861) that she thought her heart would break when she said goodby to her dear friends, to her sisters, and to her little daughter, Lizzie, whom she left with Julia Campbell.

The last few days in Bristol were the most painful of my life. Before I left, my friends gathered about me, and I believe truly lamented my departure. The children's school teacher, Miss Hannah, was very much pained to part with them. I feel as if I could never cry again. All the tears I have shed when the children's little school fellows bade them good-by. There were no silent tears, but actual howlings filled the air. You cannot imagine the trial all this has been to me. I can be stoical and bear my own sorrows, but the grief of my children is more than I can stand. My darling whom I left behind with her Aunt Julia bore up until the last and seemed as cheerful as possible, but when we kissed her good-by, she entirely broke down. I left her actually shrieking in her grief. I can't tell you how many people accompanied us to the landing. Loo called it my funeral procession, for they were all crying, the corpse more than anyone else. Mrs. Landreth, who is just as sweet and good a person as lives, took us to the landing in her carriage. Poor Major [the children's dog] ran along with the children, evidently knowing something to be wrong. And the last thing I saw while the boat steamed away was Major held by two or three boys, and the last thing to be heard was the crying of the children on the shore, and mine in the boat responding.[41]

Everywhere she went the people were mad with excitement. The firing on the flag at Fort Sumter had roused a feeling nothing but blood and war could subdue.

The strongest democrats of a week ago are the most ardent anti-Southerners now. "The flag! The flag!" is the universal cry. You find it streaming from every church window, borne in the hand of every child, elevated above the cross of the church steeple.[42]

As she came into Virginia she found the bridge posted with sentinels. From Alexandria on, soldiers and officers of the Southern states filled the cars. Realization of the extent of her own misfortune and that of the nation swept over her. "God help our poor distracted country! War of course is inevitable. A horrible, desolating civil war."

When she reached Richmond she found it alive with soldiers and "bristling with bayonets."[43] Robert had received none of her letters telling him she was coming; so when she arrived with all the children and trunks, no one was at the station to meet her. She hired a carriage and drove to the Exchange, where the Tylers usually stayed when they were in town. Happily her husband had come in from the country an hour before and was at that moment in the hotel. Priscilla sent him word a lady wished to see him. When he entered the room and found her with Robbie in her arms and the little girls around her, he was for a moment speechless with joy and astonishment. Immediately he began to make plans to send them to the safety of Sherwood, his father's home in the country, for the Union forces were rumored to be already on the march to Richmond.[44]

9

WAR YEARS

1861-1865

After the turmoil and anxiety of the weeks just past it must have seemed very peaceful at Sherwood. Julia and John Tyler welcomed the outcasts with great kindness and sympathy and assigned them comfortable quarters in the rambling white house. As Priscilla sat with the family on the back veranda, talking quietly and watching the children playing under the oaks and the boats going up and down the James River at the foot of the grove, it was hard to realize that in Richmond, only thirty-five miles away, she had seen the city beside itself with fear and confusion. Orchards in bloom, thriving gardens, and fields green with spring belied the threat of war and famine.[1]

She seized the first opportunity to relieve Mary Grace's anxiety in regard to her safe arrival:

Sherwood Forest
Virginia
May 28, 1861

Here I am, my dearest Mary, in a haven of safety at last, after going through oh! so much trouble and excitement and sorrow. I am wrong to say in a haven of safety, for Father last night was telling us all, my family and his, that we would most probably be obliged to fly from here at a few moments' notice, for the enemy are approaching us on either side. Father's place at Washington has already been ruined, he fears, and the fighting will be all around us. The mail from the North has been discontinued entirely, and I cannot hear from my dear child, Lizzie, or from Loo and Julia about arrangements of different kinds they were to make for me.

I cannot tell you all I suffered in parting from Bristol, not the people but from my home. . . . I thought my heart would break at bidding adieu forever to the home of my lifetime, even though it is situated in a state that has disgraced and degraded itself as Pennsylvania has. I have no Northern feeling or love for the North, but I do love Bristol; and it is tearing my very heart strings to part with it, though no consideration could have induced me to remain there when Robert was forced away.

Oh, Mary, how terrible these times are, Richmond and Washington both bristling with bayonets. I saw a S. C. Regiment pass the hotel while I was there. Such a splendid looking set of men! With a bouquet, thrown by the ladies, upon every bayonet. . . . Every man you see is in uniform. Even Father talks of fighting.

I suppose we shall be obliged to go from here soon. I very much fear that Mr. Tyler will go into the army. He is exceedingly anxious to do so himself, and Father also wants it. The thought of it gives me the greatest agony, and it will be the last drop in the cup of unhappiness I have been obliged to drink. I try to think of the many wives and mothers around me who have equal cause for uneasiness, but nothing can reconcile me to the idea of his being endangered.[2]

Just as the Ex-President predicted, it was not long before the quiet of that pleasant retreat was disturbed by the booming of cannon, and the peaceful James was filled with gun boats. In the early years of the war, before—as Sherman phrased it—it was fought "professionally," there was a notion among the Union generals that if Richmond, now the capital of the Confederacy, were taken, the war would be over. In July, 1861, McDowell with 30,000 Union soldiers led the first of a series of attacks on the Confederate Capital. With flags flying and the sound of martial music, he jauntily started on what he thought was to be a triumphant march. At Bull Run, General P. G. T. Beauregard and Joseph E. Johnston stopped him with such emphasis that the repercussion of the shock jarred Washington.

Robert Tyler did not fight in this battle; he had refused a commission in General Custis Lee's brigade, organized to defend the city. Swords, epaulettes, and millinery of war were not for him—a man of forty-four. Until the army had greater need of him, he worked hard and faithfully as Register of the Treasury in an office in the Confederate Capitol.[3]

After McDowell's defeat, confidence throughout the South mounted. Believing that Richmond was safe from attack, Robert Tyler felt that it was possible to have his family with him in the city. They were there when his father arrived for a meeting of the Provisional Congress in January, 1862. Julia Tyler followed almost immediately—earlier than she had planned, because of a disturbing dream she had of her husband. She found him apparently well enough to sit through the first sessions of the convention and receive callers, but the following night he had a spell of dizziness which alarmed her. Robert slept on the sofa in his room at the hotel, and was present to take care of Julia two days later (January 18, 1862) when John Tyler died. He did not live to see the tragic conclusion of the war fought in defense of the principles in which he believed but left the world while there was hope of their triumph. Eulogized by the governor of Virginia, the legislature, the President and Vice-President of the newly organized Confederacy, he was laid to rest in Hollywood Cemetery beside the grave of President Monroe.[4]

His widow was desolate. The eldest of her seven children, David Gardiner Tyler, was fifteen; the youngest, Pearl, a baby of two. She did not wish to leave her home and servants to the mercy of the Union Army and hesitated to run the blockade to New York, where she could find safety in her mother's home. Protected by the guard McClellan placed around Sherwood, she felt comparatively secure but lonely and forlorn without her husband.[5]

She found in Robert and Priscilla kind friends when in the spring of '62 she and the children fell ill with an epidemic fever of some kind. Her mother and her brother could not cross the lines to come to her; it was Priscilla who came, hurrying down from Richmond, and stayed to manage the house and nurse the invalids till Julia was able to take charge again.[6]

By April the family at Sherwood were well. Priscilla, Robbie, and the girls returned to Richmond in time to share in the terror that seized the city. The battle line was only twenty-five miles away, and General McClellan had brought up the James River 115,000 soldiers and a fleet of gunboats to Drewry's Bluff, within seven miles of the Confederate capital. Richmond would fall unless General Joseph E. Johnston could prevent that catastrophe. Soldiers in grey poured into the city in a steady stream. Every one capable of bearing arms was pressed into service. Robert shouldered a musket and went to fight as a private with Lee's brigade. Priscilla, terrified for his safety, turned, as she often did when she needed reassurance, to the thought of Mary Grace, far away in Alabama:

Richmond
April 18, 1862

I have been so very unwell, my dearest Mary, for the last four or five weeks that I have not been able to write to you or go to you as I probably should have done ere now. . . .

I have never felt so worried and excited in all my life—not knowing what to do. The enemy descend upon every side and a terrible battle that my soul sickens at the thought of is pending in a few days, perhaps in a few hours. The result is only known to our Father in Heaven, and Oh! may he grant us success and the power to beat back "the insolent foe." When I think of the rivers of blood that must flow in a few days from now, my heart sinks and faints within me. Our soldiers, our noble soldiers, travel-worn and weary, have been arriving here from Manassas and going down to Yorktown for the last two weeks. Thousands and tens of thousands of them have passed within a few yards of our door.

Every encouragement that waving handkerchiefs, smiles, tears, and prayers could give them . . . bunches of flowers, and kisses blown from fair fingers they have received. And sometimes warmer words and wishes than are usual upon a first acquaintance.

Imagine Grace, for instance, with all her reserve, beckoning a young lieutenant from the ranks of the gallant Georgia 7th, leaning over a bank, handing him a bunch of flowers and saying with the tears flowing over her cheeks, "God bless you. I shall pray for you every night."

He with a look of earnest gratitude, "While you ladies do the praying, be sure we shall do the fighting." Then joining his ranks and looking back at Grace till his column passed out of sight. . . .

I have heard the Yankees are not in Fredericksburg but just opposite it. I also hear that Johnston says that they can't beat him on the peninsula by any possibility. We have already turned them from the strong position they sought to occupy and have eighty thousand men, all in good spirits and fine fighting order.

We have all been making sandbags all day. Richmond is in great excitement, every lady making sandbags.

God bless you all. All at the North are well.[7]

McClellan's host came on relentlessly until, when they were in sight of Richmond, they were beaten back. General Johnston was wounded in the encounter, and General Robert E. Lee replaced him. The Union army, floundering with heavy equipment on the muddy roads, bogged down into inactivity—at least for the time being. For some months there was good news everywhere in Virginia; from Lee against McClellan on the peninsula; from Jackson and Longstreet, who completely outwitted Pope at the Second Battle of Bull Run. In December of that year Lee made Burnside look foolish at Fredericksburg, defeating 120,000 men with little more than half that number.

People began to say the South could not be conquered; and the general public, bewildered by rumors and counter-rumors, hoped that the war was almost over. In the capital of the Confederacy, even in Mrs. Davis's brilliant drawing rooms, there were those who held sanguine opinions—but not President Davis; he was not optimistic. Nor did victories near at hand blind Robert Tyler to the seriousness of the situation in the Mississippi Valley. Every day he talked with his brother, Major John Tyler, Assistant Secretary of War, whose office was near his, and so was better informed than most people about what was actually happening in the West. Before McClellan started his march on Richmond in the spring of '62, General Grant had besieged Fort Donelson on the Tennessee River and after its surrender had gone on to capture Nashville. Within a few weeks his army was again on the move with intent to cut one of the great arteries of the Southern transportation system, the Memphis-Chattanooga Railroad. Grant was surprised at Shiloh, twelve miles from the Mississippi line, by Albert Sidney Johnston and Beauregard, and defeated them in one of the bloodiest battles of the war. Obviously the Union forces were hacking away at the supply line, both rail and waterways. When New Orleans fell into their hands on April 24, it seemed fairly clear that a few more Union victories of the kind would paralyze the Commissary Department of the Confederate Army so that it could not supply the fighting men with food, clothing, blankets, medicine, or ammunition.

Already there was a scarcity of everything, and prices were soaring. In June, 1861, one dollar of Confederate money was worth a dollar in gold, but month by month there had been depreciation, which the expedient of printing paper money only accelerated. Profiteers scoured the country in all directions buying up all the goods in distant cities and in country stores[8] until by May, 1862, boots were thirty dollars a pair; ladies' shoes, fifteen dollars; coffee, $1.50 a pound; tea, ten dollars a pound; and houses that rented for $500 annually were $1,000.[9] Mr. Petigru said that in the Confederate capital one took money to market in a basket and brought home what it bought in a pocket book.[10]

Knowing that economic conditions were likely to grow worse, and realizing that he had no resources other than a salary of $3,000 a year, paid him by the Confederacy, Robert determined to do the expedient thing: to take Priscilla and the children South. The move was dictated by economic considerations, not by fear of physical danger, for Lizzie—no less dear than the other children—was left with her Aunt Letitia Semple in Virginia.[11] Robert accompanied them as far as Marietta, Georgia, where they stayed for a time with Priscilla's brother's family. Jim Cooper was not there, for he was fighting with the Confederate army. Priscilla went the rest of the way to Mary Grace's without her husband's protection.[12]

For this information we are indebted in a round-about way to Louisa Cooper, who, far off in New York, was the best-informed member of the family as to what went on among those dear to her in the South. She was apparently one of the few people in the country who got her mail regularly. How she did it she told no one, but she received and sent a steady stream of bulletins, entirely indifferent to the consequences.

Born and bred in Pennsylvania, she was of all the Coopers the only one given to outbursts of violent hatred of the Union. On one occasion she wrote to Mary Grace of public behavior on her part which might have caused serious trouble: "In church I never pray for the President of the United States but always for the President of the Confederacy; never say 'Amen' to the war prayers. . . . I had the pleasure the other day to grind in the dust a United States flag which I found on the ground, blown from some window."

Her attitude is all the more remarkable since Allan Campbell, with whom she lived, was engineer in charge of harbor defenses, and, completely loyal to the Union, would never have countenanced such treasonous sentiment. None of the letters she received have been preserved; so perhaps she burned the originals promptly, taking care that in case of search, nothing could be found; but before she did, she carefully transcribed items she thought would interest Julia Tyler's mother, who lived on Staten Island. It is largely to Mrs. Gardiner's foresight in saving the notes Louisa Cooper wrote her that we are indebted for sufficient information about Robert and Priscilla to piece together a fragmentary story of them and the family in wartime.

When Louisa Cooper wrote to Mrs. Gardiner the letter of September, 1862, Priscilla had apparently just arrived in Marietta. She could not have stayed long there, for by May 12, 1863, she is settled enough in Alabama to be calling on Mrs. Jefferson Davis in Montgomery. She wrote to Julia Tyler, the widow of the Ex-President, passing on flattery she thought might please her.

> I went to see Mrs. Pres't Davis while in town [Montgomery]. She was extraordinarily gracious, affectionate, and you should have heard her speak of your own sweet self, or as she called

> you, "my beautiful stepmother." She could not take her eyes off you; you positively did not look one day over 20—so fresh, agreeable, graceful—dress fit so exquisitely. She could not talk to you because she just wanted to watch you. In fact, she was extravagant in your praise. But I assure you Mrs. D. did not find it half so impossible to converse as she represented, as I really thought her one of the most charmingly entertaining persons I ever met with.[13]

The cheerful tone of this fragment may have been due to the fact Priscilla had found at Longwood with Mary Grace the sense of security she had been seeking and possibly an additional bulwark of defense against the dangers which threatened, in the person of John B. Scott, a suitor for Grace's hand. Priscilla had known the Scotts ever since she first visited Mary Grace. Hardly a letter had passed between the two sisters without references to John or his mother and sister. He was of all the men she knew the one she would have chosen for her romantic seventeen-year-old daughter. He was as practical as she was impractical, as reticent as she was outgoing. He was, besides, wealthy and a

The Scotts had been originally Virginia people who had estab-

gentleman.

lished themselves in South Carolina in 1770. General John Scott (1773-1839) was the founder of the family in Alabama. He moved first to Augusta, Georgia, and then to Milledgeville, where he built the Capitol. He came to Montgomery in 1808 to claim a tract of land left him by his father. Friendly to the Indians, who were impressed by his striking and majestic appearance, he grew wealthy and added more and more plantations to his holdings. He married Eliza Coleman, of Augusta, and was said to be the father of the seven tallest, handsomest men in the country. As generous as he was prosperous, he gave to the city of Montgomery Scott's Free Burial Ground, now Oakwood Cemetery, and to the Methodist Church the property where the Post Office now stands. Like many Virginians, he was an Episcopalian, and St. John's enjoyed from him liberal gifts and continued support. He had built with slave labor the substantial plantation home just down the road from Longwood, to which John Baytop Scott, his grandson, wished to bring Grace as a bride.[14]

When Priscilla had arrived some months before with her children, John had just been invalided home from the army and was making a slow recovery from illness. He was frequently at the Raouls', completely fascinated by Grace's beauty but rather baffled by her behavior. Feeling herself to be admired, she tried to behave as the fragile heroines did in the innocuous novels her mother let her read. She cultivated a little way of putting her hand to her heart and sinking onto a sofa, saying, as she did so, "Je suis fatiguee."

When she had gone through this performance on several occasions, the puzzled young man asked Priscilla, "Why is Miss Grace always so tired?" Priscilla laughed and told him the little goose was trying to impress him with one of the few French phrases in her limited vocabulary.[15] As soon as he realized that it was not he who wearied her, John went about his courting in earnest and won her for his own.

After the wedding in November of 1863 Grace settled down happily at Fairlie—as John's old home was rechristened. Letty, Tousie, and Julia were content to be left with the Raouls; so Priscilla felt free to go back to Richmond with her husband, taking her baby, Robbie, with her. Fortunately for Grace Tyler Scott, Mary Grace was just across a meadow and through a stretch of woods; the pretty bride did not know a single useful thing about housekeeping. She delighted John by putting a flower in her hair when she went about her duties, carrying her little basket of keys like a badge of office. She asked questions of him, the well-trained servants, and the competent matrons who came to call until she knew enough to please her husband.[16]

She tried to live up to her new duties as a married woman and behaved with dignity as chaperone to her elder sister, Letty, when John took them both to the "starvation parties" at Mt. Meigs, where the young people got together to frolic. It was considered bad taste to serve refreshments at these gatherings, but laughter and games were free. Never for a moment could the war be forgotten; but when the soldiers came home on furlough, the women and girls tried to put their anxieties aside and show them smiling faces. Sometimes there was a tournament in John's grove; and the young men competed to see who, riding with wooden lance atilt, could gather the largest number of rings suspended on the branches of the trees. The victor would crown his lady Queen of Love and Beauty and sit with her at the head of the table spread with the meagre picnic supper. The knowledge that these boys would soon be engaged in real battles, not such mimic warfare, keyed the young people up to a high pitch of excitement. Poor Letty, robbed of a carefree girlhood by the war, made the most of these occasions. Her mother, seeing in Richmond the hysterical gaiety of war-time young people and fearing for her own girls, wrote an unnecessary warning to her dignified eldest daughter.

May 4, 1864

I received your letter, my dear child, yesterday and was truly rejoiced to see your handwriting and so long a letter from you telling me that all my dear ones were well. Give my tender love to all, not forgetting my son, John. Aunt Peggy and all returned to Tarwood on Tuesday, but I have no doubt but that the enemy will drive them in again today or tomorrow. The town is full of rumors of all kinds. The Yankees are all advancing in great force from all directions, and among the troops detailed to meet them the Treasury Battalion will be ordered out, it is said.

We are all once more quite well, though Robbie still looks delicate. He has had no color since he has been here, and everyone thinks him very delicate looking. I intend having his hair cut in a few days, as it no longer curls and makes him uncomfortable.

I am glad you have had so pleasant and so gay a time at the Mount [Mt. Meigs]. I did not object to your going to Montgomery again, but only to your going the same day I did. I thought you ought to stay a week to devote yourself to Julia. Even now, my child, if you wish to go there, do not remain at the Mount on my account. I wish you to do everything you desire to promote your enjoyment, consistently with your duties and the strict propriety which should influence every action of a young girl, especially when removed from parental guardianship.

I need not fear that you will act imprudently, for your natural pride and dignity of character and heritage of what is right will keep you free from the follies, imprudences, and—I am sorry to add—the indecencies of many of the young ladies of the Confederacy. I hear wherever I go such dreadful accounts of the conduct of the girls of the various cities that I feel sometimes tempted to take you—all of you—and shut you up in a nunnery. But you are the children of many prayers, of much careful teaching and earnest love. When I am separated from you all, I commend you—morning and night to the merciful care of our Father in Heaven, and I feel that He will protect and care [for] you as well when I am separated from you as when I am with you.

May 6th

Today has been one of great excitement and trouble. The telegraph will tell you tomorrow more than I can today. The Yankees are advancing on all sides, and your dear father has been ordered out with his battalion again. Aunt Peggy and Cousins Betty and Ellen have come in again from Tarwood. The enemy have burnt down New Kent Court House, and poor Aunt Peggy has left her house and farm and servants, feeling that all may be destroyed.[17]

When Priscilla wrote this letter the days of the Confederacy were numbered. William Tecumseh Sherman had started his devastating march through Georgia, and Grant was beginning his Wilderness Campaign. Richmond, a besieged city, was staggering to its fall.

Apparently Robert lost no time in sending his wife and son back to the comparative safety of Alabama. Fanatically loyal to Jefferson Davis, he stayed on at his post, greatly disturbed by ugly talk about the leaders of the Confederacy, the number of deserters who went over to the enemy and the bad news from every battle front. His friend, J. B. Jones, a clerk in the War Office of the Confederacy, gives us a fleeting glimpse of him, a bit "edgy" with an acquaintance, Foote, formerly United States Senator from Mississipi, now a Confederate Congressman.

Sept. 29, 1864

As I walked down to the department, heavy and brisk cannonading below assailed the ear. It was different from the ordinary daily shelling, and to my familiar senses it could only be a

BATTLE. The sounds continued, and even at my desk in the department the vibrations were very perceptible.

About 10 o'clock, when walking down Main Street (the cannon still heard) I met Robert Tyler and Mr. Foote, member of Congress, the latter in some excitement, denouncing the management of the Executive. He said if Richmond were lost he should move that the people take matters into their own hands, and proclaim a *dictator*. Mr. Tyler, commanding his temper, banteringly told him he ran some risk of being arrested, tried by drum-head court martial and shot—before night. Mr. Foote whirled away, repeating his desperate purpose; and Mr. Tyler repeated more gravely that he might be arrested for treasonable language—and ought to be.

Mr. Tyler then invited me to join him at breakfast at a neighboring restaurant, where we had each a loaf of bread, a cup of coffee with milk (but brown sugar), and three eggs. The bill was $16.[18]

Later as Grant battered hard against Lee, who defended Richmond, Jones wrote:

The battalion of clerks still remains at Bottom's Bridge on the Chickahominy. The pickets hold familiar conversation every day with the pickets of the enemy, the stream being narrow and crossed by a log. For tobacco and the city papers our boys get sugar, coffee, etc. . . .

Robert Tyler has been with the Departmental Battalion at Bottom's Bridge, doing service as a private, though the head of a bureau.[19]

The war had reached Alabama by the beginning of April, 1865. Priscilla wrote to her sister-in-law in Virginia, Mrs. Letitia Semple, a dramatic account of the coming of Wilson's Raiders to Mt. Meigs.

August, 1865

My dearest Letty:

Once again let me try to write to you. I have written over and over again by mail and private hand since last April, but I know you could never have received my letters, or I should have heard from you and my darling Livy before now. The only way I have heard from you is through Loo from New York, from whence she sent me your letter to her. I heard first from Mr. Tyler in the same way. I have heard only twice from him by letter for eight months. My life has been spent in such cruel anxiety and uncertainty that sometimes I wonder that I live. God has been very good to me in sustaining my health. This has enabled me . . . to bear all the terrors and unhappiness through which we have passed. We have each, dear Letty, a terrible experience to relate when we meet of the last few months since April. I seem to have lived ages.

About the beginning of April, hearing that Wilson's army of Raiders was approaching Montgomery, John sent Grace, Letty, and Tousie to Newnan, Georgia, and Mary sent Theus and Tom's wife to Atlanta. John Scott and Frederic were both enlisted in a volunteer company for the defense of Montgomery, and expected to be marched out with forces thirty miles below there to meet the enemy.

Mary and I were left alone. She remained at home with Julia, and I stayed in John's house to protect his property if possible. When the girls left us, it was reported that the Yankees were within five miles of Montgomery. So you may imagine the distress and excitement. We buried our valuables at one o'clock in a dark wood, and set our houses in order, expecting we scarcely knew what horror before we met again. The alarm proved a false one; and a week passing over quickly, dear Grace was determined to see John again and came back from Newnan by herself in the cars—a journey of twenty-four hours. She arrived, very tired, at four o'clock in the afternoon and resolved she would not leave home again, happen what might.

The same night John arrived home from his post, hearing she was at home, dreadfully disturbed at her coming, the enemy being but a few miles from Montgomery. She was obliged to go in an open carriage with broken-down horses and a weak, wretched conveyance with Charlie Cooper, the driver, the cars having made their last trip in the night.

I never saw such a countenance of helpless misery as hers as she left the house, supposing she might never see her house or husband again and not knowing what might be my fate. It would take a volume to describe that journey she took to Newnan through horrible swamps, over shocking roads, her carriage breaking down, hundreds of vehicles before and behind them, mules dying in the swamp . . . and the poor darling seized with chills, fever, and the most wretched headaches. Her horses balking, the harness breaking, and everything around her being too miserable to think of.

She left here as much misery as she took with her. The authorities decided not to defend Montgomery; so John at one o'clock Tuesday drove off with three gentlemen [to take] their stock to some safe place. Frederic did the same. Mary and I were left to our loneliness.

Tuesday night the whole sky was lighted with the burning warehouses in Montgomery—hundreds of thousands of bales of cotton. About ten o'clock some Confederate officers rode up, wearied and wretched, to John's house for a night's lodging, they being the last of our army in Montgomery, having remained there to set fire to our stores. At daybreak they rode off, and then I felt lost indeed.

The Yankees took possession of Montgomery the same morning. The whole road was full of wagons, carriages, men, women, and children flying from town they knew not where. All Wednesday night we saw different blazing spots on the horizon in every direction. I supposed them to be the various country houses near Montgomery. They did not reach the Mount until Thursday morning, when parties of twenty, fifty, etc., walked out here, seeking what they might devour. In some places they behaved horribly, as much so as possible. A brute came to Mary's house and behaved in the most dastardly manner, putting a pistol to her head and demanding her gold, silver, etc.; then getting a coal of fire and threatening to burn her house down if she did not give him money. She was dreadfully frightened but could give him nothing. After cursing and flying out in the greatest rage, he left, stealing only a horse.

I determined when I heard her story to walk down to their camp three miles off to get a guard or protection for John's house. I set off by myself, with a prayer to God for protection. When I walked about a mile and a half, I met a squad of men with an officer riding at their head, whom I halted. I told my errand, informing him of the infamous manner in which his men were frightening the women and children, all the men being away. I happened upon the very man to help me, the Adjutant General of Wilson's command, a Mr. Latla from Philadelphia, who knew Mr. Tyler very well. He was very polite, gave me a very strong protection paper, ordering his men not to enter our houses on pain of death.

Fortunately when I got home no Yankees had been there; and they did not come until late in the afternoon, when about fifty walked into the gate and through the back of the house—as desperate a looking set as ever lived. After I displayed my paper the officer was quite polite and only demanded some bacon. . . . The same day three sets came, upon whom my paper worked wonders. The day was bearable, though I cannot describe the excitement I was all the time in. I kept the house all locked up and I remained on the back piazza all the time. When night came on I realized I was all alone in the house. I thought sometimes I should die.

Every night the horizon was lighted by fires. I never undressed for three nights. I always sat up till two or three o'clock. Upon paper this all looks like nothing but it was a living death.

There was a calm about a week after Wilson passed through. And we began to find out all the damage the fiends had done, the property they had destroyed. Poor John suffered dreadfully. They went to his plantation four miles from his house, burnt a nice house there . . . twenty-five hundred bushels of corn, took quantities of meat, all his dry . . . (he had a quantity), all his peas . . . rice; in fact all his provisions or nearly all. The meat they left they divided among his servants.

J. set up a saw mill with two cousins of his about a day's journey from Montgomery, near Pensacola. Grace will not move down till they build some houses. The location is healthy and the country abounding in game, fish, oysters, etc. I hope the change will benefit her health. She is very thin and exceedingly changed from the blooming and lovely girl of two years ago.

Goodbye, my dearest Letty. Whenever you communicate with James give (him) my truest love. I always feel as if he was my real brother.

And may God bless you both.
Kiss dear Bessie for me.

Ever yours,
Faithfully and affectionately,
E. P. T.[20]

She saved the home; but the plantation storehouse in the prairie, where all the meat, the seed, and the supplies were kept, was destroyed. Robert Tyler in a letter written after the war says that John Scott lost in slaves and at the hands of raiders property valued at $100,000—a fortune in the '60's.[21]

These stirring events took place in early April, 1865, so the letter says. On April 2, 1865, Grant's men came swarming over the breastworks that protected Richmond. All hopes for the

Confederacy were over. Robert Tyler followed his President to the last ditch. He was dismissed by Davis in the old mint at Charlotte and made his way to Danville, where he surrendered to the United States authorities. After a brief stay in Richmond he rejoined his family in Alabama, having lost everything but his honor and the love and respect of those who knew him best.

While he was in Richmond he received a letter from Buchanan, saying that although he had never approved of his stand in favor of the secessionists, he had never questioned the sincerity of his motives. He enclosed a check for $1,000.[22] Robert's reply was no less generous and noble, but he returned the check. His letter, written on August 13, 1865, sounds as if there were no fight left in him, only submission to God's will:

> . . . the conflict is now over and I bow my head in humble submission to the will of God. My political race is ended and my destiny is fixed. I shall devote the rest of my life to work and dedicate my remaining energies exclusively to my wife and children. The War has left me literally *nothing,* but an unstained honor that has triumphed over the many temptations of my life and the many weaknesses in my character, and a resolute will. And daily it requires greater patience of mind and temper to look out on the prospect before me with an unblenched cheek. But God in this hour helps me to do that.[23]

Robert Tyler was weary when he wrote that letter, but his desire to serve the public good would return when he saw the chaos that Reconstruction brought to Alabama. He had no more real desire to give up political conflict than the salamander, born in flame, wishes to escape the fire.

10

RECONSTRUCTION IN ALABAMA

1865-1877

There seems little to choose between the hopelessness which follows hope and the hopelessness which follows despair; yet they mount like a spiral stairway, round on round, till aspiring man attains the spiritual triumph of resignation and courage. At the close of the war Priscilla wrote to Julia Tyler that she felt numb after all she had gone through and looked upon herself as "dead and buried"; that she felt less like a living woman than a stone image, a "monument" to her former self. She was surprised that she continued to go through the motions of eating, sleeping and performing the usual tasks.[1]

Slowly and painfully she achieved sufficient perspective to accept her personal losses and the defeat of the Confederacy as final and to go about the reorganization of her life. The obvious thing for Robert to do was to open a law office in Montgomery and acquire a practice as quickly as he could. Penniless and middle-aged, he must undertake to compete with half-starved professional men, who, like himself, were beginning life all over in a land bled white by four years of conflict. Immediately after his arrival in Alabama in 1865 the Tylers settled down to an existence lacking in comfort but not without consolations—at least, that seems the impression he wishes to convey when he wrote to his good friend, Ex-President Buchanan, on March 16, 1866.

. . . My family (of whom you are kind enough to enquire) resides in the country about 15 miles away. I have opened a law office in this place and am trying to earn a respectable support. The Legislature has recently passed a Stay-Law, however, that I fear will prove disastrous to the profession. You must know that I have become the most economical person of your acquaintance—neither drink, smoke, or chew—never enter a club or theatre—in truth, am a self-supporting machine—sweep my own floor, make my own fires, cook my food, clean my shoes, fetch my water, and serve myself in all particulars except to wash my clothing. I sleep on a cot in my office. On Saturday evening I go into the country to see my family and remain with them until Monday morning.

Mrs. Tyler and the children manage to live very economically but without a positive deprivation of the necessaries of life on a place near Mt. Meigs in this county. Letitia teaches the younger children and a half dozen other little boys and girls. The gentleman, Mr. John B. Scott, to whom my daughter Grace is married, was wealthy before and during the war, but lost more than a hundred thousand dollars during the last few weeks by the cavalry raids and by the sudden emancipation of his slaves.

I have reason to be thankful to God that I did not lose any of my immediate family during the war, and that my children are without exception obedient, truthful, and amiable and worthy of my devoted affection. Their excellent mother has moulded their characters and has done her duty in this as in all other things.[2]

The end of the war had left the Southern states bankrupt politically, socially, and economically. They existed in chaos, without a government except that implied by military garrisons. The Freedmen's Bureau gave help to thousands of Negroes and poor whites that first hard winter, but in spite of this fact many were without food or shelter, and many died of starvation after the failure of the crops that year.[3] When Priscilla heard the tales of destitution, especially distressing in the northern part of the state, she counted herself as fortunate that she and her family had a warm welcome at Fairlie. John Scott was happy to have them there, for Grace was expecting her first child, and he did not wish her to be alone while he was forced to be away during the day supervising the work in the outlying fields.

Wilson's raiders and wandering bands of marauders had stripped him clean of implements, seeds, and stores; he had no cash to pay wages or buy fertilizer, but he still had land—more than he could cultivate or pay taxes on. A few of his Negroes, like his body servant, Charlie Cooper, had never left the place; and many of the older and less aggressive who had gone away in the first ecstasy of freedom came wandering back to be fed and cared for. Although the Freedmen's Bureau encouraged them in habits of laziness by giving free assistance and a great deal of advice about how to treat the Southern white, many of John's former slaves wanted to go back to the security of life under their old master, and a few of them were willing to work. John accepted them—good and bad alike—as part of the inherited burden the institution of slavery had laid upon him. Partly for their sake and partly because he knew no other way of life than depending upon seed time and harvest, he put in his crops. He was doubtful of profit, for although there were no state taxes in 1865-1866, there was the Federal levy of fifteen dollars a bale on cotton, which in spite of several years of crop failure sold at a price so low as to mean his ruin.[4] However, the future seemed no more desolate than the years just past. After he had been invalided home from the army he had raised what was needed as food by his family and those dependent upon him. No one on the plantation had gone hungry. While many of his neighbors had only peas and bacon, molasses and cornbread, he had usually managed by skillful farming to vary this monotonous diet; for his fruit trees bore and his garden flourished. As soon as it was reasonably safe, he began to add to the scanty herd of cattle, the few geese, chickens, and turkeys he had kept hidden in the swamp where the raiders could not find them. He had always been what the Black Belt calls "a good provider"; so even now, though he suffered as did those about him at the hands of pilfering Negroes and poor whites, he usually had in the storeroom or smokehouse something from which Priscilla could achieve a tempting dish for her husband when he came from Montgomery each week end.

Robert Tyler looked tired and worried. He seldom brought good news from Capitol Hill, and after Grace and the children had retired, he, Priscilla, and John usually talked politics far into the night. Frederic Raoul, Tom Taylor or some other man from one of the neighboring plantations frequently joined these sessions, for Robert's deeper knowledge of government and his personal experience in Washington and Pennsylvania made him a minor oracle to the group. There was in the spring of 1865 plenty to talk about. In May of that year President Andrew Johnson issued his Proclamation of Amnesty, the provisions of which excited some indignation but little surprise. It was in the main a continuation of Lincoln's policy, already familiar—except that it excluded from pardon all those with taxable wealth of $20,000 or more, as well as those who had held office in the Confederacy or borne arms against the Union as high-ranking officers. With one sweeping gesture it disfranchised those Southerners who did not receive pardons, and rendered many of the former governing class in Alabama helpless to correct abuses of their personal rights or those of their country.

In July, 1865, the President named as provisional governor Lewis E. Parsons, who had been on both sides during the War.[5] Conventions were held that fall, and by the following December Alabama had a regular governor and a legislature recognized by the President. It seemed to Robert Tyler and those with whom he discussed public affairs that law and order were in the process of being restored—though it was not a law and order of their choosing. The people of the Confederacy did not expect to be welcomed back into the Union, but they were not prepared for what followed. When the Alabama delegates, together with those of the other newly organized state governments, presented themselves in Washington, they were denied seats in the House and in the Senate.

By their exclusion a strong radical group of Republicans, led by Stevens and Sumner, challenged the President and inaugurated a struggle for power, which was soon to disrupt temporarily the delicate balance of authority among legislative, judicial and executive branches of the nation. Consternation swept the South as it became evident that this powerful coalition in Congress had its own plans for reconstruction, different from Lincoln's or Johnson's, and far more vindictive.

There are no family letters to describe the shocked surprise felt when the Civil Rights Bill was passed over Johnson's veto in March of 1866, giving "equal rights to citizens of every race and color." It was followed a year later by the Reconstruction Act of March 2, which imposed unrestrained Congressional rule and a military dictatorship upon the defeated South. A desperate letter from Priscilla to her daughter Letty, who had gone to Fernandino to teach school, indicates that life in Alabama had become intolerable to her.

> I think that everything now is as bad as it can be . . . I have just come from Montgomery. . . . The town reminds me of descriptions I have read of St. Domingo in its most populous parts. Negro women sit along the sidewalks with their baskets of provisions while the men fill the street. They never move an inch to let a lady pass and actually at times I walk into the streets to get around them. They are dirty and ragged, looking unhappy, restless and hungry. But few white men are to be seen in the street, and those, wretched and hopeless looking, burdened down by debt and uncertain as to the future. The Negro is the inhabitant of the town, the arbiter of its destinies, while over all floats in every direction the Stars and Stripes, a hollow mockery! God only knows where it will all end.[6]

What was happening on the plantation was no less disheartening. The Freedmen's Bureau, designed to exist for one year, had been continued and had become an instrument for the humiliation of the white man. It regulated the terms on which the Negro would work and brought up for trial before its courts white men who had incurred the ill will of any disgruntled black.[7] Although John Scott had no serious labor troubles, he lived in fear and dread. He would walk the floor all night after he came back from gatherings in Mt. Meigs, where an underground resistance among the planters was being organized. There he heard from other men of his kind alarming stories of the fate of those who failed to meet the recently imposed high taxes on land and all kinds of property. Those who failed to pay promptly had their plantations confiscated and could redeem them only by paying double the assessment plus the cost.[8] He had no accumulation of funds to meet this emergency; and if his land were taken from him, he could not live. Priscilla wrote frankly to her brother-in-law, Allan Campbell, who was as generous as he was rich, that John needed a considerable sum of money. Promptly there came in answer a kind letter and a check for $1,000, which relieved the immediate fears of the master of Fairlie and assured the family of subsistence until tax time came around again. In gratitude John sent Allan a magnificent silver pitcher and goblet that had been won by his father's race horse, West Wind, in the days when the Scotts could afford the sport of kings.[9]

This incident brought home to Robert and Priscilla the fact that they could no longer impose upon the hospitality of the Scotts; and since Robert found it impossible to earn a living as a lawyer in Alabama, Priscilla wrote to him on July 10, 1867, counseling flight.

> I cannot bear to think of you as unhappy. . . . Your note complains of making no money in Alabama. Do you look forward with any degree of certainty to a time when money can be made there? Have you any idea of any office there combined with your law practice? Painful as removal would be, I cannot but think you would do better to accept John's [Robert's brother's] offer of the office in Baltimore. . . . In a city Letty and Tousie might both obtain places as visiting governesses. . . . I too might procure writing. . . .
>
> If you are doing nothing and do not look forward to doing anything where you are, you can do no harm by moving away. I for myself can truly say I would rather go to the center of Africa if you could maintain yourself and be independent there.[10]

Priscilla should have known her husband better than to suggest his running away. Like the patriot he was, Robert Tyler stayed to fight on the side of the oppressed whites in his adopted state. Towards the end of 1867 he found the opportunity for which he had been looking. He accepted a position as editor of the Montgomery *Advertiser* and began actively to serve the cause to which he dedicated his best efforts during the remainder of his life.

With the power now in the hands of the nefarious Committee of Fifteen, the plans of its moving spirits, Thaddeus Stevens, Charles Sumner and Wendell Phillips, bade fair for a time to make of the conquered land a black man's heaven and a white man's hell. They succeeded temporarily in having it treated like a foreign country which the United States had conquered and garrisoned. Sumner approved the Southern states' having rights such as are enjoyed by territories of the Union; but Stevens denied that they had rights; he held that by being defeated they forfeited the constitutional protection of their lives, their liberties and their property. He even advocated confiscating the land of the ruined plantation owners and dividing it into forty-acre plots—one for each Negro.[11] There was a lack of sanity in his proceedings but no lack of shrewdness. Dying with consumption, the bitter old man ran a race with death as if to see how large a legacy of hatred he could leave behind him.

After Johnson had served his ignominious turn as Chief Executive (1865-1869), Grant succeeded him. That honest soldier was a man without guile, but he numbered among the friends to whom he was loyal racketeers, hardly to be matched for rascality; Gould and Fiske, responsible for the speculation in gold which resulted in "Black Friday," September 4, 1869;[12] Oakes Ames, a member of the House, who as one of the directors of Credit Mobilier involved the members of Congress in a tremendous swindle;[13] McDonald, whose Whiskey Ring cheated the government of revenue;[14] Belknap, Secretary of War, who lived lavishly on money taken from the post traders of the Indian Reserve.[15] In the inner sanctum of the Republican Party there was a steady accumulation of soiled linen, which, when aired, shocked the whole country.

Carpetbaggers had flocked South and scalawags were ready to take possession of the state, when on March 30, 1870, in the second year of Grant's administration, the Fifteenth Amendment put the ballot into the hands of the partially civilized black. There is no point in rehearsing the full list of the offenses of those who governed Alabama during Reconstruction nor the frauds practiced upon the "freed" Negroes to make them sustain in office officials like W. H. Smith,[16] A. J. Applegate,[17] D. P. Lewis,[18] Richard Busteed,[19] Charles Hays,[20] George E. Spencer.[21] One fantastic lie among many was that any Negro who did not vote with the Republican party automatically lost his status as a citizen and became a slave.

In the stately Capitol in Montgomery, where Jefferson Davis had taken his oath of office, a room was set aside in which lobbyists could meet and bargain with members, most of whom had their price.[22] Harrington, the speaker of the House, boasted that he received $1,700 for getting one bill passed; and a leader among the legislators, that he got $35,000 for the successful management of a railroad bond issue.[23] The state debt rose under misrule from $7,000,000 to $33,000,000, and the county and municipal debts probably proportionately as much.

Fortunately there is in the American system of government provision for the righting of the wrongs it commits. Reasonable men in this country are never entirely helpless in the face of insufferable conditions. As Robert Tyler watched the political scene, he felt born within him righteous indignation that would not let him rest. Priscilla had never been so proud of her husband as when, benefiting by his experience as party leader in Pennsylvania, he began with other men of his kind to help build the machine which was eventually to drive out the evil regime. At first, he and his associates moved as warily as Indian scouts, covering up their footprints; for they were in danger of physical violence, and all that saved them was the over-confidence of those who represented the forces against which they fought.[24]

Robert Tyler had always been passionately interested in the welfare of his country; since his earliest manhood he had taken an active part in politics, but never before had his motives been so completely free from personal ambition. He and the group with whom he worked sacrificed their time and strength and risked their lives to bring back once again decency and self-respect to the government of their state. His name does not appear in Bowers' *The Tragic Era* or Fleming's *Reconstruction in Alabama,* but the fact remains that he was editor of the Montgomery *Advertiser* from 1867 to 1874 and that during the crucial years 1872-1874 he was the hard-working Chairman of the State Democratic Executive Committee, both of which historians recognize as powerful agencies in driving the Radical Republicans from Alabama.

Shortly after he became editor of the *Advertiser,* Priscilla had moved to Montgomery. She wrote to Letty, her eldest daughter, that they had rented three rooms over a school down on Perry Street below St. John's and planned to go to housekeeping with a bed, lent by Grace, a table, a dozen sheets and pillow cases, a tin teapot, a silver milk jug, two china tea cups and a few odds and ends.[25] They were still desperately poor, but the girls were growing up and assuming the responsibility for their own support. Letty, now a handsome woman of twenty-six, was an experienced teacher, who could freeze a roomful of restless children into obedient submission by one Gorgon-like look. Tousie, fearing she never could be so capable as her elder sister, set out that fall for Baltimore to help Aunt Semple, President Tyler's daughter, at the school she had opened, called the Eclectic Institute.

In an effort to help the family Tousie went on with her work even after she was courted by Albert Taylor Goodwyn, lately Confederate officer, now the owner of Elm Hill, a fine plantation in Elmore County. The eldest son of Harriet Bibb and Albert Gallatin Goodwyn, he was connected with a roll of distinguished families—Taylors and Legares in South Carolina, Cobbs and Bibbs in Georgia. These facts were important to the Tylers—not that they were snobs, but in a society stripped of wealth, to be wellborn is a matter of moment.[26]

Albert Goodwyn was brought to call by Thomas Gardner Foster at the inadequately furnished house where the Tylers were living. Foster had been an admirer of Lizzie's ever since he had met her one Sunday in the choir at St. John's and had walked home after service with her. His father, Thomas Flournoy Foster, Congressman from the Ninth District in Georgia, had been well known to the Tylers when they lived in Washington.

Priscilla made the two young men welcome, and the girls came into the sitting room as soon as they knew there were callers. Tousie had just arrived from Baltimore and had been unpacking her trunk. She looked, she feared, "rather mussed," but Albert thought her very pretty, very gentle, very unattainable. He fell in love before the evening was over, and soon after, with Robert's full consent, proposed and kept proposing till she accepted him. They were married at St. John's Church in 1869. Foster was best man, and two years later, in April, 1871, he and Lizzie made a match of it.[27]

Julia Campbell Tyler, Priscilla's youngest daughter, had the advantage of being named for Allan Campbell's wife and being especially dear to him. He clothed her and sent her to school, and saw that she made a proper debut in New York. He was her escort when she went to her first ball, a splendid affair in honor of the Grand Duke Alexis of Russia. It was in his home that she met Harry Hewlings Tyson, son of Priscilla's oldest and dearest friend. She and Harry were married in Montgomery in April of 1874[28] and went North to live.

A great many gentleman callers presented themselves at the Tylers' while the girls were there. The house was always filled with young people, and Priscilla exerted herself to make them happy. Sometimes, if they coaxed her, she would read aloud to them—usually from Dickens's novels. She could impersonate Mrs. Wilfer from *Our Mutual Friend* in a way to make her audience roar with laughter. One day when Robert was at his office the Negro who did odd jobs around the place came running up to his desk, greatly distressed. He urged Mr. Tyler to come home, for "Ole Miss" must have heard bad news. The family were, he reported, all "crying into their pocket handkerchiefs." Robert made what haste he could, only to find that it was their mother's reading of the death of Paul Dombey that had reduced his daughters to tears.

Priscilla was in her fifties during these years, but when the girls were gone and Robert was engrossed in work, she often felt like an aged woman. A loose sheet from one of her many lost journals shows her looking back over her life as if she thought herself done with it indeed.

> What sorrows it has been my lot to bear, God only knows. What comfort and happiness I have also known through His Divine mercy. With agonies of grief I cannot describe I have parted with three lovely children—my eldest born, my Mary Fairlie, and two sons (so beautiful!), John and Cooper. Terrible as the affliction I endured when they died, I now feel content that it should be so. As I grow older, I feel nearer and nearer to them.
>
> God has given me a large family of fair and good children, who are loving and dutiful. I have six living now—one married, who has given me another object of affection and interest in a dear grandson, nearly a year old.
>
> I have been separated from my home and friends of my early years, and for seven fearful years have made my home in this state. I have passed through all the horrors of a desolating war and known the greater agony of a still more desolating and humiliating peace, if that can be called peace which this country now endures. This burden of taxation, of Congressional oppression and military rule.
>
> My dear husband has had a bitter struggle to go through—almost wishing for death after the downfall of the cause in which he was engaged; his fortunes utterly broken; without one cent. He has commenced anew as it were to fight the battle of life in his declining years for the maintenance of his wife and children. And never was man by wife and children more loved and honored than he—kind, patient, enduring, gentle, uncomplaining, full of energy and determination. I feel that God will bless his efforts.
>
> I try to emulate his example, but my health is bad, I am fretful and desponding and feel sometimes a burden to all that love me.[29]

She was, of course, nothing of the sort, but a source of strength to her husband when in 1874 the crisis came in the struggle between the Democratic Committee and the Radical Republicans. That year the Supreme Court of Alabama declared legal intermarriage between the races, and United States Senators

Morton and Boutwell were agitating the mobs to demand mixed schools. When the 4,000 white Republicans who met the representatives of the Negro clubs in Montgomery promised them the choice of nominations in the coming election, the White Man's Party rose in revolt. They nominated a ticket headed by George S. Houston, and announced that they were prepared to fight.[30]

The issues in the coming campaign were clearly stated on the editorial page of the Montgomery *Advertiser,* February 19, 1874, as having nothing to do with party principles, but as "a contest between antagonistic races for that which is held dearer than life by the white race."[31]

The Radical members of Congress, realizing that desperate measures were in order, voted money to give relief to flood sufferers on the Alabama River that spring, and saw to it that the supplies were held over until just before the election. Doubtful Negroes were told that if they would vote the Republican ticket they would get one or two shoulders of bacon. This offer did more harm than good, for there was not enough meat to go around, and considerable grumbling was occasioned among those who had no share in the largesse.[32]

In previous elections lurid tales of atrocities committed by the whites against the blacks had been effective in maintaining the Radicals in power. Early in the year there was published in the Hartford *Courant* a series of stories about crimes committed by white men against the blacks in Alabama. The New York *Tribune* sent a reliable Republican to investigate, whose testimony branded as a liar the rascally Congressman, Charles Hays, who started the tales. Right-minded Republicans throughout the nation were embarrassed at this revelation of fraud, and Northern Democrats expressed their sympathy for a maligned people by contributing a considerable sum to the campaign fund of the State Democratic Committee. Impoverished Southerners strained every effort to give with equal generosity. As a result, the Committee was able to flood the mails with tons of literature pleading its cause. All but ten of the seventy-five lawyers in Montgomery and a proportionate number from other sections stumped every city, village and crossroads, till the timorous were ready to walk with the brave to the polls and demand and get an honest election.[33] Houston and a Democratic legislature were swept into office, and the Radical Republicans were on the run.

After this triumph for the principles in which he believed, Robert Tyler resigned the chairmanship of the Democratic Committee and the editorship of the *Advertiser,* assuming the editorship of the *News,* a less strenuous office. A kind of autumnal peace brooded over the next three years. The girls, all except Letty, were married to men of whom their parents approved; Robbie seemed destined to add new glories to the name of Tyler; the family enjoyed what in the South during the 1870's was considered a competence. They should have been happy, and so they were, in a quiet way; except that the heavy hand of mortality fell so often on those they loved: on Julia Campbell, Priscilla's sister; on Thomas Cooper Campbell, Julia and Allan's only son; on Priscilla's sister, Virginia Cooper Thorburn; on Julia Tyler's daughter, Julia Tyler Spencer; on Mary Grace's husband, Frederic Raoul. Priscilla wept over letters of condolence which she addressed to the bereaved families, recommending them to the comfort to be found in Christ. She had always been a devout churchwoman, but a quickening of faith was present in her attitude toward death.[34] She had need of spiritual strength, when, very suddenly, Robert died. He had been in court on the morning of December 3, 1877, as foreman of the Grand Jury, when he felt dizzy and asked to be taken home. By afternoon he was better and was conscious and comfortable up to the moment of his death at nine that evening.[35]

W. W. Screws, editor of the *Advertiser,* put the paper in mourning for his friend and associate. Bordered by bands of black, the editorial page was devoted to a biography and eulogy, praising Robert Tyler as a gentleman who "did not know what it was to harbor a mean thought or to be actuated by unmanly or dishonorable motives . . . too noble to cherish malice." Screws said that in the darkest days of Alabama's history Robert Tyler "never faltered in his devotion or in his hopes for her future redemption. And no man in the state did more than he to bring about this consummation."[36]

Tributes to him appeared throughout the South, stressing his leadership during Reconstruction against the enemies of good government. There was an especially eloquent editorial in a Pittsburgh paper, as if Pennsylvania wished to make tardy amends for driving him into exile.[37] Resolutions were passed by the Alabama Bar Association and by the Grand Jury.

Shortly before he died, when he was still quite well, Robert Tyler brought Priscilla a poem he had written. She did not show it to her daughters immediately after his death; but long afterwards, when she read it to them, she wept pitifully. Present-day critics would condemn it as morbid and sentimental, but it did not seem so to his wife.

When the grass grows over me,
Head to foot, where I am lying;
When not any wind that blows,
Summer's sun, nor winter's snows
Shall wake me to your sighing—
You will say, "How good he was."
You will say, "How true he was—"
When the grass grows over me.

When the grass shall cover me,
Hold me close to earth's warm bosom;
When I laugh, or weep, or sing
Ah! never more, for anything,
You will find in blade or blossom
Sweet small voices everywhere
That will speak me as I was—
When the grass grows over me.

When the grass grows over me,
Very patient I can wait,
Knowing that or soon or late,
There will dawn a clear tomorrow,
When your voice shall cry, "Alas!
Now I know how good he was;
Now I know how true he was"—
When the grass grows over me.[38]

11

OLD AGE AND DEATH

1877-1889

After Robert's death Priscilla lived twelve years. Time was kind to her, exacting the inevitable forfeitures of strength and beauty so gradually that those who loved her noticed no abrupt change. She never seemed to them suddenly less erect and slender, less quick of wit, less charming. To the day of her death she was always a most distinguished woman in any gathering and one most eagerly listened to. She went seldom into society but did not lack an admiring circle of children and grandchildren, who never forgot the elegant way in which she sat or the stately way in which she entered a room. They remembered too how devastating the effect of her satire could be when she reduced them to helpless laughter by imitating some person whose hypocrisy or pretentiousness irked her, and how great her tenderness when they turned to her for sympathy. She was in old age, as she had been in youth, a powerful personality.

Robert's unexpected death left her destitute. Her son, Robbie, charming and ineffectual; her sons-in-law, barely earning a living for their families—no one of these could provide for her. Fortunately Allan Campbell assumed responsibility for her support and took Robbie as his secretary. It was probably the first time in Priscilla's life that a strong man with an ample bank account had stood between her and the world. There was something very special in the friendship between them; she looked to him for security—one of the most vital needs of an old woman; and in her companionship he found release from loneliness for his wife, Julia, and sorrow for his son, who had died the same year Robert did (1877). Priscilla spent every summer with him, and they kept up a lively correspondence during her absences.

During the early years of her widowhood she spent the winters with Mary Grace, who had seen her through all the vicissitudes of her life. The old ladies, with their daughters Letty and Theus to look after them, lived together in a house on Columbus Street. Letty taught school in the basement. Twenty-five little boys and girls, under Miss Tyler's vigilant eyes—pale blue and myopic behind heavy glasses—studied the three R's and practiced unaccustomed niceties of behavior and articulation. Miss Letty was free with the switch and with devastating sarcasm. As grown men and women, her pupils have been known to wake up in a cold sweat from dreaming that they had incurred her wrath by dropping a final *g* or slurring the *-ed* on the past tense of a verb. Hers was a kind heart and a noble character, but her effect upon the young was terrifying.

Neither Letty nor Theus wasted time in bewailing their spinsterhood. They were always busy—Letty with the school, and Theus with such projects as becoming a photographer, a painter, or a musician. She was never bored, for though she mastered none of the arts, she was always happy to begin a new one. She had for some years a dancing class, and Mary Grace patiently strummed polkas and waltzes while all the children in the family connection tried to emulate Theus's grace on the ballroom floor.

The two old sisters, dressed alike in widow's weeds, wearing caps edged with ruching on their white hair, looked on with approval as their fine daughters struggled to improve the minds and manners of other people's children. They lamented, of course, the fact that the men who might have been the husbands of these spinsters had perished in the war. They worried a great deal about their futures but had more immediate cause for distress at the wretched struggle of their married children, who were trying to keep their heads above water in the backwash of the war. By the time John Scott, Albert Goodwyn, or Thomas Raoul had paid the taxes, he would find there was nothing left to meet the note due at the bank for last year's supplies. The transition from plantations cultivated by slave labor to farms run by Negro share-croppers was disastrous to the landowner, who found himself caught up in an economic situation that threatened his survival.

Tousie could not bear to see her husband burdened with debt and anxiety. She had—as the phrase goes and the psychologists deny—"inherited" her mother's histrionic powers. Being far less fragile and helpless than people thought her, she determined to use her talents to relieve the wretchedness of their situation. With her mother's help she secured engagements for a series of readings in the East. George W. Childs, editor of the *Public Ledger* in Philadelphia, made the arrangements there;[1] and in New York Priscilla's cousin, Mrs. James Roosevelt, and Allan Campbell were in charge. After the recital in New York Mrs. Roosevelt gave a reception, and Priscilla stood with Tousie to receive the compliments of her old friends on her pretty daughter's accomplished performance. The trip was socially, artistically, and financially a great success. Albert looked at his wife with considerable amazement and increased respect when she returned with good Yankee dollars to put into the Goodwyn treasury.

Those of Priscilla's sons-in-law whose livelihood did not depend upon the price of cotton were more prosperous than the others—Harry Tyson, clerk of a court in New York City; and Gardner Foster, manager of the newly organized gas company in Montgomery. Lizzie's home at 531 South Perry Street became the mecca for all the country boys and girls—Grace's six and Tousie's five children. There they enjoyed a taste of city life—quite shy and awkward in their homemade clothes until they were thawed by the kindness of their aunt and uncle. In the summer the situation was reversed, when Gardner, Jr., Henry and Priscilla Foster visited at Elm Hill and Fairlie. Their grandmother was determined that the Tyson children should not miss the fun of playing with their Southern cousins; so on her yearly trips she would take an Alabama child or two to spend the summer in New York.

Virginia Scott, Priscilla's eldest granddaughter, used to tell how seriously her mother, Grace, studied fashion plates and how desperately she ran the sewing machine in order to send her North with her adored grandmother in what Mt. Meigs thought was the latest style. The little country girl was assailed by self-conscious fears that her costumes were not quite *a la mode* when they visited the Biddles in Philadelphia, but felt quite at home after they reached Allan Campbell's four-story brown-stone house, 125 Lexington Avenue. There Louisa, Priscilla's youngest sister, was the housekeeper. Grown quite stout, she sat in the sitting room upstairs and let the servants and guests follow their own inclinations. She would not leave the comforts she was accustomed to in the city, when, at the first hint of warm weather, Allan invited Priscilla, Robbie, and whoever happened to be visiting, to his cottage at Deal Beach. As they sat rocking on the porch in the cool sea breeze, the two old folks never seemed to run out of absorbing topics of conversation. Robbie devised fascinating games for the children, wrote plays and music for them; he was probably never so happy again in his life as when he amused his little nieces and nephews on the sands, with his mother and his Uncle Allan looking on indulgently.

This peaceful pattern of life—New York in the summer, Alabama in the winter—was disrupted in 1884 when Priscilla's daughter, Julia Tyson, died. Old Mrs. Tyson and Priscilla had a misunderstanding—painful to both in view of the unbroken friendship they had enjoyed for many years. The quarrel arose over the disposition of the three children: Louisa, Allan, and Grace. Their Uncle Allan Campbell very much wanted the baby, Grace; so Priscilla asked for her. Mrs. Tyson thought the little family should not be separated. Following Harry Tyson's death there was a lawsuit, and only after unpleasantness on both sides did the situation adjust itself in Priscilla's favor. The three children were usually with her at Allan's and spent several winters in Alabama.

Priscilla and Mary Grace grew presently too old to bother with housekeeping. Mary Grace went to live with her son, Thomas Raoul, at Longwood; and Priscilla, with Lizzie Foster. All of her devoted daughters and their husbands conspired to spoil her. When she came in the fall from New York there was a bustle of preparation at 531 South Perry Street, directed by Priscilla before her arrival:

I suppose you have had my wall papered and a chair back and arm covering made for my chair and everything else you could do for my room. Mouse traps in both rooms! Oh, have the hinge put on the door between the rooms and I will pay for it. And have my tea kettle cleaned. Make Maria come and do it all.[2]

During these years she demanded a great deal of attention from everyone—from Aunt Maria, a tall, turbaned Negro woman who spent a lifetime in the employ of the Fosters, to tiny Priscilla Foster, the most conscientious of little girls about seeing that her grandmother had ice water in an earthen jug by her bed at night.

Priscilla Cooper Tyler was seventy-three when she was taken ill in New York. She wrote the words of the Tyler crest: "Spes et fortitudo" at the top of the letter that announced her final homecoming.[3] And with courage but without hope she endured pain and suffering during the last months of her life. Mary Grace, who never failed her as sister and devoted friend, was with her when, just as the sun broke through a bank of clouds, at eight o'clock on the morning of December 29, 1889, she passed away painlessly and unconsciously.[4]

There were editorials written after her death about her eventful life. One of the most eloquent and comprehensive was that in the Philadelphia *Sun,* the author of which described himself as being "one of the silver-haired old fellows who recall her with delight as young, beautiful and talented."[5] She would have been glad to be so remembered, for even as an old woman she was not indifferent in regard to praise—not for her own sake but for that of her children. She wrote to Julia Tyler in 1870, when Laura C. Holloway was preparing a series of sketches, *Ladies of the White*

House, that she was pleased to be included. "Really," she said, "the only ambition I have left is that my girls may have some memorial written of me respecting my birth, parentage, and education that will give them pleasure and that they can show their children."[6]

In these words she gives her consent to the writing of this biography—the story of a remarkable woman who used her talents not to further a career of her own but to play an important part in the lives of three men: her father, who made her his leading lady; President Tyler, for whom she acted as mistress of the White House; and her husband, whom she left free to follow a high destiny, never quite attained.

NOTES

THE MANY REFERENCES to the letters and journals on which this biography is largely based are to volume and page number in *The Cooper Papers*. The authors of all letters and the persons to whom they are addressed are indicated in the text. Few Cooper manuscripts bear reliable dates; chronology had for the most part to be determined by internal evidence.

CHAPTER 1

1. Thomas A. Cooper added the "A" to his name to distinguish himself from Thomas Cooper, the publicist from Oxford, driven from England for his political opinions. Friends said it stood for Abthorpe or Apthorpe. Joseph Norton Ireland in his official biography, *A Memoir of Thomas A. Cooper* (New York, 1888), spelled it *Abthorpe.*
2. Stanley T. Williams, *The Life of Washington Irving* (New York, 1935), I, 89.
3. Washington Irving, *Salamagundi* (Philadelphia, 1870), p. 111.
4. These names appear throughout *The Cooper Papers* (University, Alabama, 1952), III, 74, 78, 82, 84, 87, 88; IV, 140, 142, 173, 174; etc. Dr. Hosack taught botany at Columbia until he married a wealthy woman and retired to an estate at Hyde Park. Brockholst Livingston was a distinguished lawyer; Robert Livingston was a chancellor of New York and an author of essays. J. O. Hoffman, the lawyer with whom Washington Irving studied, was the father of Matilda, beloved by Irving. The Hoffmans were, like the Bre-

voorts and the Kembles, wealthy landowners, part of the Irving circle. Gouverneur Morris was a statesman, for a time Minister to France. He was fabulously wealthy and lived on a grand scale, employing two valets and a hair dresser for his personal use.

5. Robert Yates married Jane Van Ness. Maria Yates, their daughter, married Major James Fairlie. Their children were:

   John
   Louisa
   Mary m. Thomas A. Cooper
   Julia m. Samuel G. Ogden
   Nicholas

   For information about the Yates family see n. 14, *infra.* The Van Nesses (Williams, p. 403) were an old Dutch family of distinction. Judge William P. Van Ness, Irving's friend with whom he stayed often at Kinderhook, was Burr's second in the famous duel with Hamilton. John P. Van Ness lived in splendor in Washington. Cornelius Van Ness was Minister to Spain.
6. George S. Hellman, *Washington Irving, Esquire* (New York, 1925), p. 80.
7. See *Cooper Papers,* II, 45-55, for letters from Mary Livingston and Maria Laight, in which these girls are mentioned as Mary's friends.
8. Joseph Norton Ireland, *A Memoir of the Professional Life of Thomas Abthorpe Cooper* (New York, 1888), p. 39. Stephen Price was "America's first theatrical speculator," at one time manager of Drury Lane, London. "Our first monopolist," he brought from England many European stars, and controlled their bookings and contracts not only in New York but throughout the whole country. Oral Sumner Coad and Edwin Mims, *The American Stage* (Hartford, 1929), p. 66.
9. A letter from Washington Irving to Joseph Gratz, quoted by Mildred Low, "A Lover of Good Company," *Canadian Magazine,* IX (January, 1923), 231.
10. Williams, p. 101; p. 405, n. 162.
11. Hellman, p. 80.
12. John B. Irving, "Reminiscences of a Tragedian," *Home Journal,* LCXXII (August 22, 1857), 4. J. B. Irving was no relation to Washington Irving. He was a prominent citizen of Charleston, S. C.

13. See *Cooper Papers,* II, 50, for Maria Laight's slighting comment on Joanna Cooper. She was the widow of Mr. Upson, a sea captain, when Cooper married her. Her tombstone in Trinity Churchyard states that she was thirty-eight years old when she died in 1808. There were no children.
14. Walter Blair, Theodore Hornberger, Randall Stewart, *The Literature of the United States* (New York, 1946), I, 365.
15. The following extract from the *Proceedings of its General Meetings, Published by the Society of the Cincinnati in 1867,* was among papers preserved by the descendants of James Fairlie Cooper, Major Fairlie's grandson. It was written by Robert Tyler.

"James Fairlie. Lieutenant 2d New York Regiment and Aide-de-Camp. Born in New York City in 1757. Died 10th of October, 1830. His father, James Fairlie, was a Havana merchant captain and the son of a Scotch midshipman who settled in America early in the last century. His mother, Phoebe Mitchell, was a Quaker lady of Long Island.

"In 1776, at nineteen, he was commissioned an Ensign in Colonel McDougall's Regiment, and on that officer's recommendation, on the reorganization of the army, was retained as a Second Lieutenant in Colonel Van Cortlandt's, serving with it at Saratoga. Baron Steuben, in 1778, selected him as one of his Aides, and he was with him at Monmouth on the 28th of June, afterward accompanying him to Virginia. . . .

"When the war ended he was relieved from the attendant distress which followed many officers without means of maintenance. The kind-hearted Baron offered it, in opening a home to him and employing his pen in his palace of logs, styled 'The Louvre,' erected on his granted lands in Western New York. There, with Walker, North and other visiting veterans, he participated in that hospitable 'Bachelor's Hall' until new duties successively sought him.

"He was appointed the Claim Agent for the State of New York, and a member of its Legislature in 1798 and 1808; a Presidential Elector in 1804 and 1816; an Alderman of New York City, and one of the Delegates to the memorable State Constitutional Convention of 1821, and served for many years as Clerk of the Supreme Court of this State. Jefferson conferred upon him the honorary position of Commissioner in Bankruptcy, and Madison offered him the position of Adjutant-General in the War of 1812.

"When he died, at 41 Cortlandt Street, New York City, his loss was considered a public one, and his funeral was attended by the New York Cincinnati Society, he having acted as its Secretary in 1784.

"By his marriage with Maria, daughter of Chief-Justice Yates, he had two sons, who died unmarried. His name appears on the Half-Pay Roll."

16. Louisa Tyson, an interview (June, 1951).
17. *Cooper Papers,* IV, 138.
18. Ireland, *loc. cit.*
19. *Cooper Papers,* IV, 198.
20. *Ibid.,* VII, 319.
21. C. Kegan Paul, *William Godwin: His Friends and Contemporaries* (Boston, 1876), I, 35 ff.
22. Priscilla Goodwyn Griffin, an interview (June, 1951).
23. Joe Cowell, *Thirty Years Passed Among the Players* (New York, 1844), p. 62.
24. Louisa Tyson, an interview (June, 1951).
25. Oral Sumner Coad and Edwin Mims, p. 62.
26. William B. Wood, *Personal Recollections of the Stage* (Philadelphia, 1855), p. 418.
27. J. B. Irving, *Home Journal,* LCXVII (January 2, 1858), 4.
28. William Winter, *Other Days* (New York, 1908), p. 26 ff.
29. Wood, *loc. cit.*

CHAPTER 2

1. Doran Green, *Old Houses on Radcliffe Street* (Bristol, Pa., 1938), p. 124 ff.
2. Doran Green, *A History of Bristol Borough* (Bristol, Pa., 1911), pp. 101-143.
3. The tapestries were supposed to have been woven by order of Marie Antoinette for Lafayette. They were put up for sale at a London auction which Cooper attended. He purchased two wall hangings and two pieces each for six chairs, which upon his death were divided equally among his six daughters. "Art and Nature in Africa" is the title of the piece now hanging in the home of Ellie and John Scott, near Mt. Meigs. "Art and Nature in Europe" is in the museum in Montgomery, Alabama. The others have been worn out or lost.
4. Green, *History,* pp. 101-143.
5. Green, *Old Houses,* p. 177.

6. Thomas A. Cooper married Mary Fairlie. Their children were:
   Mary Grace m. Frederic S. Raoul
   James Fairlie Cooper m. Fanny Spiers
   Elizabeth Priscilla Cooper m. Robert Tyler
   Olivia Perry Cooper m. A. McDonald
   Julia m. Allan Campbell
   Virginia m. A. Thorburn
   Louisa
   Stephen Decatur (died as an infant)
   William Gaston (died as an infant)
7. Priscilla Goodwyn Griffin, an interview (June, 1951).
8. Louisa Tyson, an interview (June, 1951).
9. *Cooper Papers,* III, 78.
10. Noah Mill Ludlow, *Dramatic Life as I Found It* (St. Louis, 1880), p. 309.
11. *Cooper Papers,* IV, 191.
12. *Ibid.,* III, 92.
13. *Ibid.,* III, 97.
14. *Ibid.,* IV, 212.
15. *Ibid.,* III, 92.
16. It is in the possession of Priscilla Goodwyn Griffin, Wawa, Pa.
17. Green, *History,* pp. 144-150.
18. Arthur Hornblow, *A History of the Theatre in America* (Philadelphia, 1819), p. 216.
19. John B. Irving, "Reminiscences of a Tragedian," *Home Journal,* LCXXII (September 12, 1857), 1.
20. Pierre Irving, *Life and Letters of Washington Irving* (Philadelphia, 1872), III, 94.
21. *Cooper Papers,* III, 73.
22. Ludlow, pp. 311-320.
23. *Cooper Papers,* III, 78.
24. *Ibid.,* III, 80.
25. *Ibid.,* III, 84.
26. *Ibid.,* III, 95.
27. *Ibid.,* III, 74.
28. *Ibid.,* IV, 197.
29. *Ibid.,* III, 76.
30. *Ibid.,* III, 82.
31. *Ibid.,* III, 88.
32. Pierre Irving, III, 25.
33. *Ibid.,* III, 97.

CHAPTER 3

1. *Cooper Papers,* IV, 138.
2. *Ibid.,* IV, 167.
3. *Ibid.,* IV, 198.
4. *Ibid.,* IV, 153.
5. *Ibid.,* IV, 212.
6. Philip Hone, *Diary of Philip Hone (1828-1851)* (New York, 1936), p. 107.

7. Joseph Norton Ireland, *A Memoir of the Professional Life of Thomas Abthorpe Cooper* (New York, 1888), p. 56.
8. *Ibid.*, pp. 89-94.
9. *Ibid.*, pp. 59-66.
10. William B. Wood, *Personal Recollections of the Stage* (Philadelphia, 1855), p. 329.
11. *Cooper Papers*, IV, 138.
12. N. Y. *Evening Post*, Tuesday, Feb. 18, 1834, p. 2.
13. *Ibid.*, Wednesday, Feb. 19, 1834, p. 2.
14. George C. D. Odell, *Annals of the New York Stage* (New York, 1928), III, 681.
15. Ireland, *Records of the New York Stage* (New York, 1867), II, 90-91.
16. Anna Cora Ritchie, *Mimic Life* (Boston, 1856), p. 88.
17. *Cooper Papers*, IV, 139.
18. Simpson was the manager of the Park Theatre.
19. Doctor Hosack was a popular physician who married money and retired to an estate in Hyde Park.
20. Mrs. Paulding was Washington Irving's sister.
21. Probably the wife of Captain Lawrence, commander of "The Wasp."
22. *Cooper Papers*, IV, 142.
23. *Ibid.*, IV, 138.
24. *Ibid.*, III, 98.
25. W. Stanley Hoole, *The Ante-Bellum Charleston Theatre* (University, Ala., 1946), pp. 34-36.
26. J. B. Irving, "Reminiscences of the Life of a Tragedian," *Home Journal*, LCXXII (November 21, 1857), 1.
27. Hoole, *loc. cit.*
28. Louisiana *Advertiser*, April 2, 1834, p. 2.
29. *Ibid.*, April 12, 1834, p. 2.
30. *Loc. cit.*
31. Ireland, *Memoir*, pp. 69-70.
32. Louisiana *Advertiser*, April 19, 1834, p. 2.
33. *Loc. cit.*
34. *Ibid.*, April 23, 1834, p. 2.
35. *Ibid.*, April 21, 1834, p. 2.
36. Frances Courtney Wemyss, *Twenty-six Years of the Life of an Actor and Manager* (New York, 1847), p. 241.
37. Ireland, *Memoir*, p. 70.
38. *Cooper Papers*, IV, 147 f.
39. Frances Anne Kemble, *Diary* (Philadelphia, 1835), II, 86.
40. *Cooper Papers*, *loc. cit.*

CHAPTER 4

1. *Cooper Papers,* IV, 199. This information is confirmed by W. Stanley Hoole, *The Ante-Bellum Charleston Theatre* (University, Ala., 1946), p. 103. He gives the dates as March 17-31, 1835.
2. Joseph Norton Ireland, *A Memoir of the Professional Life of Thomas Abthorpe Cooper* (New York, 1888), p. 70; Arthur Herman Wilson, *History of the Philadelphia Theatre* (Philadelphia, 1935), p. 684.
3. Philip Hone, *Diary of Philip Hone (1828-1851)* (New York, 1936), p. 137.
4. *Cooper Papers,* IV, 188.
5. *Ibid.,* IV, 152.
6. *Ibid.,* IV, 156.
7. *Ibid.,* IV, 191.
8. *Ibid.,* IV, 161.
9. *Ibid.,* IV, 162.
10. *Loc cit.*
11. *Ibid.,* IV, 165.
12. *Ibid.,* IV, 171. Mrs. Radcliffe and 'Monk' Lewis were members of the Gothic school of British fiction, writers of very popular "horror-piled-on-horror" romances.
13. *Ibid.,* IV, 168.
14. "Editor's Table," *Knickerbocker,* VI (October, 1835), 377.
15. *Cooper Papers,* IV, 169.
16. *Ibid.,* IV, 171.
17. *Ibid.,* IV, 169.
18. *Ibid.,* IV, 183.
19. *Ibid.,* IV, 181.
20. *Ibid.,* IV, 174.
21. *Loc. cit.*
22. *Loc. cit.*
23. George C. D. Odell, *Annals of the New York Stage* (New York, 1928), IV, 73.
24. *Cooper Papers,* IV, 175.
25. *Ibid.,* IV, 176.
26. *Ibid.,* IV, 177.
27. *Ibid.,* IV, 178.
28. *Ibid.,* IV, 182.
29. *Ibid.,* IV, 191.
30. *Ibid.,* IV, 194.
31. *Ibid.,* III, 98 ff.
32. Louisa Tyson, an interview (June, 1951).
33. This is a family legend in the Scott family. It was James Scott, Grace's eldest son, who ran away for a day.
34. *Cooper Papers,* IV, 195 ff.
35. Ireland, *Memoir,* p. 71.
36. *Loc. cit.*
37. *Cooper Papers,* IV, 203.
38. *Ibid.,* IV, 196.
39. *Ibid.,* IV, 214.
40. *Ibid.,* IV, 213.
41. J. B. Irving, "Dr. Irving's Reminiscences of the Charleston Stage," South Carolina *Historical and Genealogical Magazine,* II (October, 1950), 201.

42. *Cooper Papers,* IV, 209 ff.
43. Doran Green, *Old Houses on Radcliffe Street* (Bristol, 1938), p. 163.
44. *Cooper Papers,* IV, 213.
45. *Ibid.,* IV, 197 ff.
46. Anna Cora Ogden Mowatt, *Autobiography of an Actress* (Boston, 1853), p. 378.
47. Arthur Hornblow, *History of the Theatre in America* (Philadelphia, 1919), p. 151.
48. Ireland, *Memoir,* p. 76.
49. Albany *Argus,* October 28, 1838, p. 2.
50. J. B. Irving as quoted in Ireland, *Memoir,* p. 77 f.

CHAPTER 5

1. *Cooper Papers,* IV, 208.
2. Tylers mentioned in *The Cooper Papers:*
John Tyler
m. Letitia Christian
Mary m. Henry L. Jones
Robert m. Elizabeth Priscilla Cooper
John m. Martha Rochell
Letitia m. Jas. A. Semple
Elizabeth m. William Waller
Anne Contesse lived 3 months
Alice m. Rev. H. M. Dennison
Tazewell m. Nannie Bridges
Another child that died in infancy
m. Julia Gardiner
David m. Mary M. Jones
John Alexander m. Sarah Gardiner
Julia m. William H. Spenser
Lachlan m. Georgia Powell
Lyon G. m. Annie Tucker
Sue Ruffin
Robt. Fitzwalter m. Fanny Glin
Pearl m. William M. Ellis
3. *Cooper Papers,* IV, 209.
4. *Ibid.,* V, 223.
5. *Ibid.,* V, 230.
6. *Ibid.,* V, 223.
7. *Ibid.,* V, 222.
8. *Ibid.,* V, 218. No copy of this volume is available. *Ahasuerus* (New York: Harper and Brothers, 1842) is signed "By a

Virginian." Robert Tyler used a pseudonym, for he shared the aristocratic prejudice against publication felt by most Southern gentlemen. There is a family legend, unauthenticated, that Poe praised this work highly. Robert Tyler wrote likewise *Medora's Dream,* of which no copy can be found.

9. *Ibid.*, VI, 247.
10. See Note 8 above.
11. *Ibid.*, V, 218.
12. *Ibid.*, V, 226.
13. *Ibid.*, V, 234.
14. *Ibid.*, V, 224.
15. *Ibid.*, V, 226.
16. *Ibid.*, V, 234.
17. *Ibid.*, V, 238.
18. *Ibid.*, VI, 247.
19. Laura C. Holloway, *The Ladies of the White House* (Philadelphia, 1881), p. 318 ff.
20. Kate McLemore, *Kith and Kin* (Montgomery, 1948), p. 74 ff. Raouls mentioned in *The Cooper Papers:*
    Caroline Eliza Theus
    m. John Paul Thompson (1771-1810)
    m. Jean Rose Marie Desire Raoul de Champmanoir of Dinan, France
    Caroline m. Thos. T. Stark (remained at Belleville)
    Louis m. Eliza Huger
    Alfred m. Eliza Hassell
    (Both Louis and Alfred came to Alabama)
    Harriott Pinckney m. Dr. Tom Burge Taylor
    (They lived at Chantilly near Mt. Meigs, Alabama)
    Frederic Sebastian m. Mary Grace Cooper
21. *Cooper Papers,* VI, 258.
22. Oliver Perry Chitwood, *John Tyler* (New York, 1939), p. 6.
23. *Cooper Papers,* VI, 252.
24. *Ibid.*, VI, 261.
25. *Ibid.*, VI, 256.
26. *Ibid.*, VI, 266.
27. *Ibid.*, VI, 268.
28. *Ibid.*, VI, 274.
29. *Ibid.*, VI, 266.
30. Chitwood, p. 203.

CHAPTER 6

1. Charles Dickens, *American Notes* (New York, 1914), p. 98.
2. Mrs. E. F. Ellet, *Court Circles of the Republic* (Hartford, 1869), p. 296 ff.
3. *Cooper Papers,* VII, 286.
4. The New York *Herald,* August 24, 1841, as quoted by Oliver Perry Chitwood, *John Tyler* (New York, 1939), p. 389.
5. Chitwood, p. 256.
6. *Ibid.*, p. 228 f.
7. *Ibid.*, p. 318.

8. *Ellet,* p. 307 ff.
9. *Cooper Papers,* VII, 286.
10. Priscilla Cooper Tyler, as quoted by Ellet, p. 305.
11. *Cooper Papers,* VII, 286.
12. *Ibid.,* VII, 285.
13. Priscilla's nose turned up just enough to be called "impudent." The family teased her about it.
14. *Cooper Papers,* VII, 286.
15. Chitwood, p. 394.
16. Chevalier de Bacourt, *Souvenirs of a Diplomat* (New York, 1885), p. 191.
17. *Ibid.,* p. 209 f.
18. *Ibid.,* p. 214 f.
19. Chitwood, p. 394.
20. de Bacourt, p. 256.
21. *Cooper Papers,* VII, 296.
22. *Ibid.,* VII, 293.
23. *Ibid.,* VII, 298.
24. *Ibid.,* VII, 307.
25. *Ibid.,* VII, 303.
26. *Ibid.,* VII, 300.
27. Dickens, p. 106.
28. *Ibid.,* p. 105.
29. The New York *Herald,* March 20, 1842.
30. *Cooper Papers,* VII, 308. "Boz" was Dickens's pen name.
31. John Adams, as quoted by William Perrine, "When an Actress Was Mistress of the White House," *Ladies Home Journal* (October, 1904), p. 15.
32. *Cooper Papers,* VIII, 323-333.
33. Mrs. Robert Tyler as quoted in Laura C. Holloway, *Ladies of the White House* (Philadelphia, 1881), p. 330.
34. Chitwood, p. 386.
35. Louisa Tyson, an interview (June, 1951).
36. *Cooper Papers,* VII, 313 f.
37. "News of Long Ago," Alexandria *Gazette,* January 12, 1843, p. 2.
38. *Cooper Papers,* VII, 319 f.
39. *Ibid.,* VII, 317 f.
40. Chitwood, p. 325.
41. *Ibid.,* p. 397 ff.
42. *Ibid.,* p. 391.

CHAPTER 7

1. They were for many years in the possession of Virginia Scott Coleman.
2. *Cooper Papers,* IX, 342 f.
3. Oliver Perry Chitwood, *John Tyler* (New York, 1939), pp. 372-385.

4. *Cooper Papers,* IX, 343.
5. Chitwood, *loc. cit.*
6. Joseph Norton Ireland, *A Memoir of the Professional Life of Thomas Abthorpe Cooper* (New York, 1888), p. 78.
7. *Cooper Papers,* IX, 343.
8. *Ibid.,* IX, 342.
9. *Ibid.,* IX, 346.
10. *Ibid.,* IX, 358.
11. This fragment is among unpublished papers in the possession of Sue Ruffin Tyler.
12. Julia G. Tyler writes to her mother, Dec. 16, 1855 . . . "He [Robert Tyler] tells me among other things that his wife has help'd herself to a sewing machine, which Singer let her have for $60. Being *who she was* he let her have it for half price. . . ." There are several similar references to Priscilla's family pride. See *Cooper Papers,* XI, 451 f.
13. Ireland, *loc. cit.*
14. James E. Murdock, *The Stage or Recollections of Actors and Acting* (Philadelphia, 1880), p. 374.
15. This pronouncement in regard to butter and the account of his interest in cooking is a family legend, substantiated by Murdock, *loc. cit.*
16. Louisa Tyson, an interview (June, 1951).
17. Lyon G. Tyler, *Letters and Times of the Tylers* (Richmond, 1885), II, 449.
18. *Cooper Papers,* IX, 348 ff.
19. "The Minutes of the Primary Society of Promoters," in possession of Frank Charles, Chantilly, Mt. Meigs, Alabama.
20. *Cooper Papers,* IX, 353.
21. *Ibid.,* IX, 362.
22. *Ibid.,* IX, 361.
23. *Ibid.,* IX, 353 f.
24. Tyler, II, 645.
25. *Cooper Papers,* IX, 374.
26. *Ibid.,* IX, 375.
27. *Ibid.,* IX, 358.
28. Ireland, p. 79.

CHAPTER 8

1. Priscilla Cooper Tyler was baptized Elizabeth Priscilla, but signed herself E. P. Cooper or P. E. Cooper, depending on impulse. Priscilla, her daughter, named for her mother, renamed herself as soon as she could talk. President Tyler gave her a pair of red shoes and told her the story of "Goody Two Shoes." Thereafter Priscilla tried to call herself after the

heroine of the tale, but could achieve nothing closer than "Tousie." Of the many Priscillas among her descendants a number have been called by the nickname.

2. *Cooper Papers,* X, 398.
3. *Ibid.*, XI, 451.
4. *Ibid.*, X, 401.
5. Oliver Perry Chitwood, *John Tyler* (New York, 1939), p. 10.
6. *Cooper Papers,* X, 396.
7. *Ibid.*, X, 393.
8. *Ibid.*, X, 421.
9. *Ibid.*, X, 406.
10. *Ibid.*, X, 395.
11. *Ibid.*, X, 409.
12. *Ibid.*, X, 410.
13. Julia Scott Gunter, an interview (June, 1951).
14. Van Wyck Brooks, *The World of Washington Irving* (New York, 1944), p. 26.
15. *Cooper Papers,* X, 414.
16. *Ibid.*, X, 416.
17. *Ibid.*, X, 419.
18. Louisa Tyson, an interview (June, 1951).
19. *Cooper Papers,* X, 422.
20. "Allan Campbell," an obituary in the New York *Tribune,* March 18, 1894. Grace Tyson Gatewood contributed the clipping and the story of Julia's crossing the Andes.
21. *Cooper Papers,* X, 437.
22. Lyon G. Tyler, *Letters and Times of the Tylers* (Richmond, 1885), II, 505.
23. Philip Gerald Anchampaugh, *Robert Tyler, Southern Rights Champion* (Duluth, 1934), pp. 74-142.
24. Tyler, II, 526.
25. *Ibid.*, II, 560.
26. Anchampaugh, p. 143.
27. *Cooper Papers,* XI, 454.
28. Anchampaugh, p. 344 ff.
29. Doran Green, *A History of Bristol Borough* (Bristol, 1911), p. 55.
30. Louisa Tyson, an interview (June, 1951).
31. *Cooper Papers,* XI, 459 ff.
32. *Ibid.*, XI, 466 ff.
33. "Allan Campbell," New York *Tribune,* March 18, 1894.
34. *Cooper Papers,* XI, 472.
35. *Ibid.*, IX, 380.
36. Anchampaugh, pp. 306-314; 313-315.
37. *Ibid.*, p. 312.
38. *Cooper Papers,* XI, 480.

39. Doran Green, *Old Houses on Radcliffe Street* (Bristol, 1938), p. 151.
40. *Cooper Papers,* XI, 487.
41. *Ibid.,* XI, 488.
42. *Ibid.,* XI, 484.
43. *Loc. cit.*
44. *Loc. cit.*

CHAPTER 9

1. Sherwood is standing, and is still much as it is described here. After considerable family litigation it is now in the possession of J. Alfred Tyler, the grandson of Julia Gardiner and President John Tyler and son of Judge D. Gardiner Tyler. As long as the plantation was within McClellan's lines the General had a guard stationed there; but the withdrawal of his army left it a prey to the troops of less well-intentioned officers. After Mrs. Tyler went to join Mrs. Gardiner in New York, vandals destroyed a great deal of furniture and burned all the family papers. The mansion was used towards the end of the war as a school for white and colored children. Sue Ruffin Tyler, in an interview (June, 1951).
2. *Cooper Papers,* XI, 489.
3. Philip Gerald Anchampaugh, *Robert Tyler, Southern Rights Champion* (Duluth, 1934), p. 341.
4. Oliver Perry Chitwood, *John Tyler* (New York, 1939), p. 464 ff.
5. *Loc. cit.*
6. Mrs. Gardiner wrote to Louisa Cooper in May, 1862: "Julia speaks of her extreme illness and ascribes her restoration and that of her family to the kindness of Mrs. Tyler. . . ." This fragment was found among unpublished letters at The Lion's Den, the late Lyon Tyler's home.
7. *Cooper Papers,* XII, 506.
8. Mary Boykin Chestnut, *A Diary from Dixie* (New York, 1929), p. 88.
9. J. B. Jones, *A Rebel War Clerk's Diary* (Philadelphia, 1866), p. 78.
10. Chestnut, p. 284.
11. *Cooper Papers,* XII, 508.
12. *Ibid.,* XII, 507.
13. *Ibid.,* XI, 485.
14. *Ibid.,* XII, 509.

15. Col. Thomas Scott emigrated from County Cumberland, England, to Gloucester Co., Virginia. He moved to Caroline Co., Virginia (1771). He married Anne Baytop.

Thomas Scott's second son, James Scott (1728-1776) moved to Prince Edward Co., Virginia, and in 1770 to South Carolina. Married Frances Collier.

James Scott's fourth son, Colonel (often called "General") John Scott (1773-1839) married Eliza Coleman in Augusta, Ga.; moved to Milledgeville (1804); built the Capitol; and came to Montgomery (1808).

John Scott's eldest son, Thomas Baytop Scott (1800-1854) married Martha Gaines Marks.

Thomas Baytop Scott's eldest son, John Baytop Scott (1831-1894) married Grace Tyler. Dr. and Mrs. William Carter Stubbs, *A History of Two Virginia Families Transplanted from County Kent, England* (New Orleans, n. d.), pp. 153-162.

16. Priscilla Scott Marks, an interview (June, 1951).
17. *Cooper Papers,* XII, 511.
18. Jones, p. 294.
19. *Ibid.*, p. 229.
20. *Cooper Papers,* XII, 515 ff.
21. Robert Tyler, a letter in the collection of the late Lyon G. Tyler.
22. *Loc. cit.*
23. *Loc. cit.*

CHAPTER 10

1. *Cooper Papers,* XIII, 530.
2. Robert Tyler, a letter in the collection of the late Lyon G. Tyler.
3. Walter L. Fleming, *Civil War and Reconstruction in Alabama* (Cleveland, 1911), p. 279.
4. *Ibid.*, p. 472.
5. *Ibid.*, p. 350.
6. *Cooper Papers,* XIII, 533.
7. Fleming, p. 438.
8. *Ibid.*, p. 578.
9. In the possession of Julia Tyson Gatewood, an inheritance from her Uncle Allan.
10. *Cooper Papers,* XIII, 531.
11. Fleming, p. 340 f.
12. Claude G. Bowers, *The Tragic Era* (New York, 1929), p. 272 f.

13. *Ibid.*, p. 396-404.
14. *Ibid.*, p. 466 f.
15. *Ibid.*, p. 474 ff.
16. Fleming, pp. 735; 591 f.
17. *Ibid.*, p. 736.
18. *Ibid.*, p. 754.
19. *Ibid.*, p. 744.
20. *Ibid.*, p. 749.
21. *Ibid.*, pp. 755; 760.
22. *Ibid.*, p. 739.
23. Bowers, p. 362.
24. John Witherspoon DuBose, as quoted in *Alabama's Tragic Decade* (Birmingham, 1870), p. 388.
25. *Cooper Papers,* XIII, 533.
26. Priscilla Goodwyn Griffin, an interview (June, 1951).
27. Priscilla Foster Stevenson, an interview (June, 1951).
28. Louisa Tyson, an interview (June, 1951).
29. *Cooper Papers,* XIII, 532.
30. Fleming, p. 782.
31. *Ibid.*, p. 780.
32. *Ibid.*, p. 785.
33. Bowers, p. 429.
34. *Cooper Papers,* XIII, 535 f.
35. "Robert Tyler," an obituary in the Montgomery *Advertiser,* December 4, 1877, p. 2.
36. *Loc. cit.*
37. A clipping, without heading, found in a scrapbook kept by Priscilla after her husband's death.
38. The poem was among the effects of Letitia Tyler, Robert's daughter. It is inscribed: "Presented to my mother by my father a few days before his death."

CHAPTER 11

Most of this chapter is based on statements from Louisa Tyson, Priscilla Foster Stevenson, and Priscilla Goodwyn Griffin, given in interviews in September of 1951, and on stories told by Virginia Scott Coleman and other members of the family. These overlap and interlace in such an intricate fashion that they defy annotation.

1. *Cooper Papers,* XIII, 537.
2. *Ibid.*, XIV, 548.
3. *Ibid.*, XIV, 549.
4. *Ibid.*, XIV, 550.
5. Philadelphia *Sun,* January 9, 1890. The obituary was found among Jim Cooper's papers after his death.
   The obituary in the Montgomery *Daily Advertiser* appeared in the issue dated December 31, 1889.
6. *Cooper Papers,* XIII, 530.

Index

INDEX